Blow Up the Humanities

Toby Miller

Blow Up the Humanities

TEMPLE UNIVERSITY PRESS
PHILADELPHIA

TEMPLE UNIVERSITY PRESS
Philadelphia, Pennsylvania 19122
www.temple.edu/tempress

Library of Congress Cataloging-in-Publication Data

Miller, Toby.
  Blow up the humanities / Toby Miller.
    pages cm
  Includes bibliographical references and index.
    ISBN 978-1-4399-0982-9 (cloth : alk. paper) —
ISBN 978-1-4399-0983-6 (pbk. : alk. paper) —
ISBN 978-1-4399-0984-3 (e-book)   1. Education, Humanistic—
United States.   2. Humanities—United States.   3. Science and the
humanities—United States.   I. Title.
    LC1023.M56 2012
    370.11′2—dc23
                                                              2012008891

♾ The paper used in this publication meets the requirements of the
American National Standard for Information Sciences—Permanence
of Paper for Printed Library Materials, ANSI Z39.48-1992

Printed in the United States of America

2 4 6 8 9 7 5 3 1

Contents

Acknowledgments

Thanks to Jenine Abboushi, Linus Andersson, Helmut Anheier, Paulina Aroch, Claudia Arroyo, Edna Bonacich, Kylie Brass, Stuart Cunningham, Todd Dufresne, Anamaria Tamayo Duque, Marina Fe, Benjamín Mayer Foulkes, John Frow, Néstor García Canclini, Malcolm Gillies, Henry Giroux, David Theo Goldberg, Michael Gordon-Smith, Bill Grantham, Cathy Greenfield, William Greenough, Larry Gross, Larry Grossberg, Julie Hare, Stefano Harney, John Hartley, Tanner Higgin, Jennifer Holt, Sal Humphreys, Ian Hunter, Yudhishthir Raj Israr, Jay Kesan, Noel King, Micah Kleit, María Pía Lara, Randy Martin, Rick Maxwell, Philip McConnaughay, Inka Salovaara Moring, Meaghan Morris, Stephen Muecke, Chris Newfield, Kate Oakley, Annie Paul, Alisa Perren, Dana Polan, André Dorcé Ramos, Luis Reygadas, Anna Roosvall, Tom Scanlon, Carol Steiner, Mila Sterling, Will Straw, Imre Szeman, and Doug Thomas. Special thanks to Kylie, Stuart, Bill, Stephen, Dana, Randy, and press reviewers for their astute, astringent, and kindly comments on the manuscript; Mila for her art; and the people at Temple University Press who finalized production. The book was begun and finished in Los Angeles and rewritten there as well as Sydney, London, Medellín, Mexico City, Paris, Madrid, and points in between. Colombia and Mexico rejuvenated my intellect and seem to have broken my heart.

Blow Up the Humanities

Introduction

The Two Humanities

The world leadership which has come to the United States cannot rest solely upon superior power, wealth, and technology, but must be solidly founded upon worldwide respect and admiration for the Nation's high qualities as a leader in the realm of ideas and of the spirit.
—National Foundation for the Arts and Humanities Act of 1965

This is not a happy time for the university, nor one of which we university men can be very proud. Liberal arts is a decaying rump of the university with no pro[sp]ects.
—Allan Bloom, "The Failure of the University"[1]

In 1966, the 91,000 humanities graduates were already double the number of 1960 graduates. They continued to rise to almost 140,000 in 1971 and 1972. During the late 1960s, better than one in six college graduates majored in a humanistic subject—up from one in twelve in 1950 and one in ten in 1960. . . . The nadir occurred in the early 1980s: 1981–1985. After that period, humanities graduates rose to about 110,000, backtracked a bit in the mid-1990s, then surpassed the 110,000 mark by 2004.
—Roger Geiger, "Taking the Pulse of the Humanities"

There are two humanities in the United States. One is the humanities of fancy private universities, where the bourgeoisie and its favored subalterns are tutored in finishing school. I am naming this Humanities One, because it is venerable and powerful and tends to determine how the sector is discussed in public. The other is the humanities of everyday state schools, which focus more

---

1. The original says "projects." I assume this was meant to read "prospects."

on job prospects. I am calling this Humanities Two.[2] Humanities One dominates rhetorically. Humanities Two dominates numerically. The distinction between them, which is far from absolute but heuristically and statistically persuasive, places literature, history, and philosophy on one side and communication and media studies on the other. It is a class division in terms of faculty research as well as student background, and it corresponds to the expansion of public higher education and the way that federal funding fetishizes the two humanities away from more prized forms of knowledge. It must end.

I wrote the initial draft of this book in a little over two months after waking up on what some people call Christmas Day and thinking, "There's a book here. It's called *Blow Up the Humanities.*" Then I thought, "That's cheeky." But as with most projects, I realized that various bits of pontificating I had done over the years had contributed to this mildly epiphanic moment.

What do I know about the humanities, both One and Two? For those who think experience matters, or who like interdisciplinarity, I have taught humanities and social sciences at a variety of locales: a military-officer training institution, several big public universities, and large private secular and religious ones. I have done so as an adjunct, assistant, associate, full, and even "distinguished" professor, in four countries and two languages, and as both citizen and foreigner. I have studied and taught in long-distance mode, from Australia to Chile to Brazil, as well as participated in the face-to-face privilege of New York University and the University of California. I have taught full time in communication studies, cinema studies, American studies, Latin American and Caribbean studies, sociology, English, and women's studies and been an adjunct in sociology, history, journalism, Australian studies, and social and political theory. I have had contracts that were not renewed in sociology and media studies.

And I have worked as a radio DJ, newsreader, sports reporter, and popular-culture commentator, in addition to jobs as a speechwriter, cleaner, merchant banker, security guard, storeman-packer, ditchdigger, waiter, forester, bureaucrat, magazine and newspaper columnist,

---

2. Although this division is particularly acute in the United States, it applies to other countries as well.

blogger, podcaster, journal editor, youth counselor, research assistant, suicide counselor, corporate consultant on culture, social-services trainer, and secretary. I have adjusted my portfolio, as it were, in accordance with changing economic conditions—as well as acted in ways that are far from professionally instrumental.

I also recently collected my third nationality. In the last week of 2009, I became a U.S. citizen. Along the way, I learned some things about the humanities in this country—supposedly a key entry point to citizenship. To be anointed as a gringo, I had to swear repeatedly under oath that I was not a member of the Communist Party—in fact, at the citizenship ceremony, just three weeks after my formal test of civic knowledge, I was required to assure a federal judge that I had not joined the party in the interim.

This was alongside promising that I had never sought to undermine another country's government. How odd, given that doing so has long been U.S. policy. Think of Lebanon, Indonesia, Iran, and Viet Nam in the 1950s; Japan, Laos, Brazil, the Dominican Republic, Guatemala, and Bolivia in the 1960s; or Portugal, Chile, and Jamaica in the 1970s. All these countries saw elections rigged or governments destabilized by the United States. Whatever.

To pass the civics test, I had to know U.S. geography, culture, demography, and politics. This started me thinking about the fact that many academics deride students for their lack of basic knowledge about the world. When I last taught in Australia, almost twenty years ago, my colleagues routinely lamented how ignorant the young were in contrast to others of some lost golden age. After I moved to the United States in the years immediately after the fall of European state socialism, it was fascinating to encounter Russian grad students in New York who had been schooled in the USSR and understood the infrastructure and Constitution of U.S. politics in ways that outdid anyone born or growing up here.

Educators often blame this dire situation on the media, which they set up in opposition to themselves (tacitly admitting, in the process, how poor they are as teachers by comparison with television sets and electronic games) (see, for instance, Lasch 1979: 226–28). In 1974, the professional miserabilist Allan Bloom divined that "young Americans no longer like to read, and they do not do so. There are no fundamental books which form them, through which they see the world and educate their vision" (1974: 59). A slew of studies seeking to account for the alienation between college students and their professors places the blame for student disinterest on popular culture, especially television, which is held responsible for "prolonged immaturity" (Bauerlein 2006: B8). Britain's Association of Teachers and Lecturers surveyed eight hundred of its members on this subject in 2009 and gleaned the following:

> 66 per cent said that *Big Brother* [2000–] was the programme that caused most poor behaviour among pupils, closely followed by *Little Britain* [2003–2006] at 61 per cent and *EastEnders* [1985–] at 43 per cent. Staff say these programmes led to general rudeness, such as answering back, mimicking, using retorts and TV catchphrases (mentioned by 88 per cent), and swearing or using inappropriate language (mentioned by 82 per cent). Aggressive behaviour was highlighted by 74 per cent of those surveyed, and sexually inappropriate behaviour by 43 per cent. ("Inappropriate Behavior" 2009)

Those pesky students. If only they had been reading a drug addict like Coleridge or Sartre, a philanderer (Augustine, maybe Byron?), or an anti-Semite—Pound or perhaps Gide.

In any event, my citizenship exam had a hundred test questions, available for study in advance. Any ten could be asked on the day, and I needed to get at least six correct. I had assumed that if you just offered some combination of "liberty," "freedom," "capitalism," "Washington," and "Lincoln," you would pass. It was more complex than that. I was ignorant of things I should have known, such as the number of amendments to the Constitution (but then so was every native-born academic and professional I quizzed other than attorneys, though a drunken yanqui in a London pub guessed more accurately than most).

I also did not "know" some test answers that were lies or, at best, errors of fact. Some of this nonsense may be trivial. For example, it is not true that Dwight D. Eisenhower was Supreme Commander of Allied Forces in Europe before becoming president of the United States (or at least, that was not his last job). He was president of Columbia University. And it is not true that Barack Obama is the full name of the forty-fourth U.S. president; it is Barack Hussein Obama II. But perhaps it doesn't matter that, just as Eisenhower must be known as a warrior rather than an education bureaucrat, doublespeak requires that "Hussein" be airbrushed from Obama's history.

Some distortions matter a great deal, however. Did you know that three countries formed the "Allies" (that could read, of course, "the United Nations") in World War II? If you thought China, Canada, or the Soviet Union were involved, you would be wrong in the eyes of the U.S. Bureau of Citizenship and Immigration Services. No, the war was won by Britain, the United States, and—France. So, leaving to one side the notable contribution of many other nations, there was no Battle of Stalingrad, and twenty million and counting Soviet citizens did not lose their lives in what they called the Anti-Fascist War. Those gutsy French did it.

Clearly, the humanities need to do some work to improve the test. And citizenship is just a subset of that labor. The humanities in the United States provide an intellectual switching point between what are often thought of—and occasionally described—as barbarism and civilization. In other words, they are a site for distinguishing class, religion, and nation. I want to short-circuit the switch and lay waste to the system.

That is a major task, especially as the law of the land decrees that "the humanities belong to all the people of the United States" (National Foundation on the Arts and the Humanities Act of 1965). Could my book's title be seditious under the terms of that legislation? Perhaps not: We might understand "blowing up" not just in an incendiary way but as a *ballon d'essai* in need of inflation. The title has certainly drawn some powerful reactions. A flight attendant quizzed me about my intentions after reading the table of contents over my shoulder before takeoff; a dinner guest said I was trying to do her out of a living; and a best friend and coauthor responded to my op-ed on the topic with a febrile letter to the editor that called me, in a rather Presbyterian moment, "unhelpful."

But these are propitious times for blowing up the humanities, whether by bombing or breathing, because their future is a very public matter. The *New York Times* avows that "economic downturns have often led to decreased enrollment" in the sector, and the global financial crisis has us sprawling in its wake. Indeed, the humanities' share of students stands at 8–12 percent of the nation's 110,000 undergraduates. That's less than half the figure from the 1960s and the lowest point since World War II, apart from Ronald Reagan's recession (P. Cohen 2009).[3] The Republican Party's Study Committee announced its desire to exterminate the National Endowment for the Humanities (NEH) in 2011 (Skorton 2011) at the same time that the American Academy of Arts and Sciences trumpeted a new Commission on the Humanities and Social Sciences (http://www.humanitiescommission .org), featuring underpublished academics from fancy schools, private- and public-sector education bureaucrats, Chuck Close, and Emmylou Harris (Berrett 2011c). I am so glad I live here.

Roger Geiger's (2009) investigation of the Academy's Humanities Indicators Project discloses a boom in enrollments during the 1960s, along with the general expansion of higher education and limitations on women's access to professional degrees. A few people from fancy universities thought they discerned renewed undergraduate interest in the late 1980s but were quickly proven wrong (Levine et al. 1989: 1).

Downturns in student interest align with two phenomena: prolonged recessions, such as those generated by Republican administrations from Reagan to the George Bushes; and an emerging passion for seemingly instrumental study areas such as business and government, especially in public schools designed for the proletariat and the middle class. Between 1970 and 2005, business enrollments increased by 176 percent, and communication and media studies (Humanities Two), by 616 percent. Language and literature both declined. The last decade has seen Humanities One account for approximately 8 percent of majors nationwide, with over half the students graduating from Research One schools[4] and little liberal arts colleges (Geiger 2009; New-

---

3. There is some dispute over the percentages. Some sources say humanities majors accounted for about 8 percent of graduates in 2009; others say the figure is closer to 12 percent (Berrett 2011a).
4. Research One universities offer doctorates and the full range of research and teaching, and their faculty must undertake research as a basic and central part of their work.

field 2009: 273; F. Oakley 2009: 36, 38). These influences have pushed colleges and universities toward vocational interests. Even those little liberal arts colleges, which have been dying off since the 1970s in terms of both absolute numbers and proportional significance, now produce graduates mostly in vocational areas. They face "evaporating wealth, slipping educational achievements, and a political environment that is sometimes hostile to higher education" (Carlson 2011; also see Blumenstyk 2010).

The following are some pertinent shifts in national enrollment figures between 1970–1971 and 2003–2004 (Chace 2009):

- English: from 7.6 to 3.9 percent of majors
- Other languages and literatures: from 2.5 to 1.3 percent
- Philosophy and religious studies: from 0.9 to 0.7 percent
- History: from 18.5 to 10.7 percent
- Business: from 13.7 to 21.9 percent

Martha Nussbaum (2009) frets that the humanities are increasingly viewed as "useless frills" and are "rapidly losing their place in curricula, and in the minds and hearts of parents and children." Some say today's public intellectuals come from science rather than letters (Wright 2010). And Imre Szeman (pers. comm., 2011) is led to ask, "Why is it that we once needed a humanities, and now we seem not to?"

Not everyone connects these trends to the proletarianization of higher education and fiscal crises caused by Republican incompetence and bipartisan imperialism. A former president of Wesleyan and Emory Universities suggests the decline happened as a consequence of "the failure of English across the country to champion, with passion, the books they teach and to make a strong case to undergraduates that the knowledge of those books and the tradition in which they exist is a human good in itself." He laments a focus on "secondary considerations (identity studies, abstruse theory, sexuality, film and popular culture)" (Chace 2009). Leaving aside the notion that books are somehow irrelevant to these latter topics, and vice versa, and neglecting this arch arch-bureaucrat's Olympian claim that such aspects are "secondary," we might legitimately inquire, as my parents did in directing me away from studying English, why students need to be in the classroom to gain the benefit of these tomes, why English is a greater "human good" than other options, and indeed how it is a "human good."

Then there are the voices of critique raining down from outside, effectively parodied by a president of the American Historical Association:

> We're the parasites, who don't bring in large outside grants that help to cross-fund other departments and disciplines. We're the pedants, who don't produce anything that can help society solve its pressing problems. We're the superfluous men and women, whom hard-pressed university administrators have to support even though our politicized scholarship and teaching has led to a calamitous loss of student enrollments, and neither they nor their trustees nor anyone else can quite see why they need to do so. (Grafton 2011)

And of course, in the context of very public disputes about opening up social history and comparative literature, "we" are also accused of failing the mission of uplift that supports a heritage of Western imperialism, Judeo-Christian ethics, slavery, representative democracy, and liberal capitalism.

Despite these claims, the turn away from the humanities is largely a result of economic crisis and enrollment surges in public universities. The vast growth in higher education from the 1970s has taken place among the lower middle and working classes. They enroll in state schools that are more vocational than private ones, and their supplies and demands are necessarily distant from narcissistic fantasies of small sections and ethical self-styling—worlds away from the arch arch-bureaucrat, who recalls his own salad student days as a period of "self-reflection, innocence, and a casual irresponsibility about what was coming next" (Chace 2009). This happy-go-lucky sophomoric *jeunesse* was described eighty years ago as "a certain degree of leisure and a favored cultural status" en route to "the professions" (Wooster 1932: 373). How very jolly.

Nowadays, of course, the tradition of Western civilization, that hybrid we are meant to teach as if it were otherwise, is not looking so good as a guide to the pursuit of life, liberty, and Facebook friends. There seems no way out of the Global North's economic crisis. Nations that grew wealthy from slavery, imperialism, war, colonialism, and capitalism are in disarray. They have quarried what they can quarry and outsourced what they can outsource. Are the humanities responding effectively to this context and associated changes to international hegemony?

I think not. Humanities scholars make grand claims about globalization, and prophets and practitioners of globalization identify culture as a core element of the process. But there is a radical disarticulation between professors, prophets, and practitioners (Davidson and Goldberg 2004: 42–43). Although culture is intimately tied to business and government, this has barely registered in the cloisters. Humanities habitués may understand the significance of culture for colonialism and imperialism, but they rarely appreciate its value to the contemporary political economy. When they do consider the latter, eyes turn and lips curl as commodity culture is contrasted with truth revealed through art or theorization (Szeman 2003). And all too often, the governing assumption is that humanities "talk need never be tested." Semiotically resistive vanguards are hailed without attempts "to nominate an agent who can act . . . [or] identify the chink in an institutional setting or situation that makes it possible to act" (M. Morris 2008: 433). Critique from beyond the center and inside the imaginary is sovereign. Action within the symbolic is not (if you need Jacques-the-Lack to get the point). And the site for a general education is turning, seemingly ineluctably, in the direction of business schools, which are characterized in the United States by an intensely reactionary vocational politics of domination (though progressive tendencies exist even within those monuments to greed; see http://www.criticalmanagement.org and http://group.aomonline.org/cms).

Samuel Weber (2009) touchingly inquires: "Do the Humanities have a future? Is there a place for the study of literature, of art, of language and of philosophy in a world progressively dominated by an economic logic of profit and loss?" Regrettably, then, we are still saddled with the shibboleth that the task of the humanities is "creative and critical thinking," understood in opposition to "science and technology" (Humphreys 2009: 9) and cultural materialism (McCloskey

2010). If those professing the humanities continue to define the field so narrowly and forget their origins, debts, and determinations, the answer to Weber's inquiry must be a resounding "No." Can you imagine his namesake or any out of Simmel, Foucault, Luxemburg, Durkheim, Engels, Trotsky, Senghor, Martí, Freud, and Marx accepting these oppositions?

A "transnational, neoliberal policy movement" has "transform[ed] the material context and framework of values in which academic research" is conducted (M. Morris 2005: 114). By and large, U.S. humanities folks have failed to make a case for inclusion in this trend—or even to admit its existence. This differentiates us from any other country I know; such is the heroic self-aggrandizement via removal from public life that is taught in graduate school here. Outside the United States, humanities intellectuals are acknowledged for a rigor that is transparent and cross-disciplinary rather than cloistered and self-regarding. In such contexts, it is normal to apply indices of quality across the sciences, social sciences, and humanities (Council for Humanities, Arts and Social Sciences 2005). For the European Science Foundation and its affiliates, creating economic vitality via the humanities, and demonstrating the fact through quantitative methods, is normal (Parker 2008). I evaluate research proposals for humanities grants from Hong Kong, Canada, the Netherlands, the European Union, Germany, Austria, Britain, Spain, Ireland, and Australia and see this tendency in very clear relief.[5] People running peak humanities bodies such as research institutes are now used to "requests from administrators, policy designers, publicists, and politicians to articulate not simply the 'value added' by the humanities to general economic well-being but also 'the metric' for making that determination" (Davidson and Goldberg 2004: 44). There are legitimate aspects to such accountability when they occur in democratic societies—and democracies are utilitarian by nature. Of course, it is equally true that

---

5. The situation of the humanities in some of these jurisdictions is far from dire, because they locate themselves inside everyday academia. So U.S. community colleges have thriving humanities enrollments, and much of the European Union sees the sector flourishing in terms of both student interest and research output (Dean Dad 2011; Committee on the National Plan for the Future of the Humanities 2009; Gillies 2010).

the way these evaluations are undertaken must always be reviewed and contested in the light of the relative autonomy researchers and teachers require from states.

Put another way, it should be uncontroversial *both* to protest a lack of autonomy *and* to seek research support. Educational and cultural leaders around the world have no difficulty explaining the significance of their institutions for public life and the requirement to be relevant to policy agendas (see, for example, Crossick et al. 2010; Dufresne 2010). We will see some of the costs and benefits of such a tendency later. I frankly find it refreshing when compared to the sorry mixture of entitlement and penury that characterizes the U.S. humanities.

U.S. humanists frequently talk about their work as if they were owed a living. That discourse derives from an extremely hidebound class, gender, and race politics, even when it is mobilized in the supposed service of progressive causes. Of course, there are historical reasons for this complex relationship between use- and exchange-value (Martin 2011). But as a consequence, ordinary people often really *hate* the humanities; or at least, they are puzzled and disappointed by them. For instance, Nicholas Dames (2011) reviewed readers' online remarks about the *New York Times*'s coverage of the 2010 collegiate killings by an Alabama biology professor—which had nothing to with the humanities—and found a triumphalist loathing of tenured faculty in our sector coming up again and again.

A self-satisfied governing cant ensures that no serious attempt is mounted to broaden either the definition of the humanities in the United States or how they are funded. The payoff from relative autonomy *should* be innovative, heterodox ideas. It is not. When I traverse the country listening and speaking, sit in editorial-board meetings, am empaneled on plenaries, read grad-student proposals, or review manuscripts for publishers, I encounter far fewer radical thinkers in the fields I straddle than is the case *anywhere else*, even as I see ever-more conventional puffery from the state about the spirit and inspiration of the humanities. We isolate ourselves by withdrawing to cloisters/enclaves of dead white men and living people of color, and the government rewards us with reduced funding. Marginalized as the keepers of a flickering flame, we seek to replace it with one that is more inclusively illuminating. We do not question the very notion of a symbolic light.

No wonder humanities journals are nativist by contrast with those in science, technology, and medicine, which have significantly higher proportions of overseas-based authors (Waltham 2010: 267). No wonder National Science Foundation (NSF) grants went from being five times the size of their NEH equivalents in 1979 to thirty-three times in 1997. Or that in 2007, the NEH received 0.5 percent of the National Institutes of Health's (NIH) budget and 3 percent of the NSF's, while in 2010, a pitiful 0.45 percent of federal research support went to the humanities. No wonder the Department of Education's policy overviews of universities essentially exclude the entire field, and Obama's 2011 State of the Union address called for increased expenditure on mathematics and science without mentioning the humanities. The 2009 American Recovery and Reinvestment Act provided not a cent to humanities research, whereas the NSF received $3 billion. The vast majority of governmental support for the humanities nowadays goes to museums, historical societies, regional regranting bodies, and libraries. The NEH typically allocates just 13 percent of its budget to universities, while private giving to the sector declined by 16 percent from 1992 to 2002. Research expenditure in U.S. universities in 2006 was $8.7 billion for the sciences and $208 million for the humanities, which are deeply dependent on universities' intramural funds—that is, tuition (Franke 2009: 13–14; Newfield 2009: 278; National Humanities Alliance 2010; Zuckerman and Ehrenberg 2009; Heitman 2011; Ellison 2009; Brinkley 2009; Yu 2008).

The conventional argument explaining this parlous situation—that the United States is a utilitarian society—simply will not fly. Given this country's economic and propagandistic reliance on culture, the humanities *are* valuable, quite apart from the fact that it is insulting and absurd to claim that other nations lack equivalently pragmatic tendencies. In Australia, an infinitely more instrumental country because it is largely undistracted by Christianity and imperialism, years of strenuous lobbying have seen the central state research body create categories supporting cultural studies and cognate fields (M. Morris 2005: 117).

Gringo humanists had better recognize the realpolitik. The toothpaste is not going back inside its erstwhile container, given the mobilization by left, right, and center of what George Yúdice (2003) calls "culture as resource." The venerable bifurcation between art and life, aesthetics and custom, literature and anthropology, has been fatally undermined by the importance of cultural property for both commerce and governance.

Christopher Newfield, an acute observer of metatrends in the humanities as well as the broader national climate, proposes "writing the future of the humanities disciplines into the funding system" (2009: 271). Newfield acknowledges that defunding the humanities has been, in part, a reaction against their centrality to critiques of state and commercial power and vocationalism. He values such critiques but suggests we should become friendlier with economic tendencies or find ourselves their hand servants—*and* watch our critiques fall flat (also see Davidson and Goldberg 2004: 45; Fish 2010b).

Such critiques fall flat in another way: They stimulate contingent labor, a phenomenon explained by Antonio Negri (2007) in resignifying the Reaganite futurist Alvin Toffler's (1983) idea of the cognitariat (also see Standing 2011). Negri uses the concept to describe people mired in casualized work who have heady educational qualifications yet live at the complex interstices of capital, education, and government. Andrew Ross explains that

> higher education institutions have followed much the same trail as subcontracting in industry: first, the outsourcing of all nonacademic campus personnel, then the casualization of routine instruction, followed by the creation of a permatemps class on short-term contracts and the preservation of an ever smaller core of full-timers, who are crucial to the brand prestige of the collegiate name. Downward salary pressure and eroded job security are the inevitable upshot. (2008: 38)

Essentially, the humanities are a cheap means of mass teaching, delivering elevation of the ruling class (Humanities One) and control of the middle and working classes (Humanities Two) at low cost. This has become a grinding tale of pain and sorrow for would-be practitioners, as those necessary tasks are taken over by other sectors.

The National Humanities Alliance (2010) describes a "jobless market" in terms of full-time employment for new Ph.D.s, with an oversupply of a thousand humanities people a year. These cognitarians typically engage in a self-exploitation and identity formation that are shrouded in seemingly autotelic modes of being, where joining a gentried poor dedicated to the life of the mind is fulfilling in itself (Gorz 2004). Their precarious nature has become central to the humanities. Tenure-track vacancies in language and literature remained static in the past forty years, even as undergraduate enrollment grew by 55 percent. In 2009, just 53 percent of humanities faculty were in full-time employment, and an even smaller proportion in tenurable positions. Compared with other fields, tenure-track hiring in language and literature occurred at two-thirds the occupational average (Geiger 2009: 4; Newfield 2009: 272; Deresiewicz 2011).

Even job candidates for tenurable lines in the humanities do not command, say, $200,000 as start-up funds with which to build their research in the expectation of large grants that will help pay for university administration, as would a scientist or engineer (Brinkley 2009). Nor will they be remunerated as though they were suffering the slings and arrows of opportunity cost by not working in corporate America. If we compare salaries in language, communications, and literature to those in medicine or economics, it is clear how cheap a humanities professor is: In 2003, health academics were paid $6,000 on average more than in 1987, during which time humanities averages declined by a thousand dollars; in 2005–2006, a business academic cost twice as much as a humanities one, compared to one and a half times as much twenty years earlier (Zuckerman and Ehrenberg 2009: 131). The relativity and flexibility are all in one direction. The alibi that economists and business professors must be paid more as part of a market loading based on opportunity costs incurred by working in universities versus corporations does not hold up. It is astonishing that the beneficiaries of these alleged comparisons with the private sector were not fired or reduced in salary with the economic crisis that began in 2007. Then again, it isn't, because the alleged market loading was never going to work like that. Nice work if you can get it:

creating the justification for increasing your salary, even as you construct the preconditions for global malaise.

Most people teaching the humanities work full time in second-tier schools with gigantic course loads, often on limited-term contracts, or they are freeway professors, traveling feverishly between teaching jobs to cobble together a living. Thousands of adjuncts each year await last-minute phone calls and messages asking them to teach large omnibus survey courses, because full-time faculty are doing their "own" work. Hiring discussions do not reference the experience of students looking for the "professor" who taught them last quarter—who did not have an office, is not back this year, and is forgotten by all concerned other than the personnel department, which has closed its files until the call goes out again for the reserve army of the professoriat to emerge from highway hell in time of need.

Clearly, there must be industrial action to counter this tendency to proletarianize working life. How might that be achieved? Democratic Party politicians, who owe so much to unions and scholars, both monetarily and intellectually, are largely ineffective defenders of labor power, while their Republican counterparts have no remorse in assaulting labor *tout court*. So we need to engage in political organizing and ideological struggle in the classroom, the corridor, and the Congress.

At the same time, we should not only be lobbying for improved working conditions. By removing our research from policy debates and applications in the name of high-minded, disembodied critique, we impoverish everything we do. The humanities needs to transcend itself to get the support it craves. Withdrawal from policy-oriented study and advocacy stimulates criticisms among the bourgeois media, politicians, bureaucrats, and corporations. They love to make fun of us for being too radical, too conservative, or too independent. I vividly recall a tired and emotional policy maker threatening to throw me off a balcony at a party when I said I worked in the humanities and social sciences. Not very nice conduct, but I suspect it happened because I was from an area renowned for its hauteur as much as its auteur.

So in answer to the question with which I began, a combination of faculty anxiety about student fitness, my citizenship experience, the delusions of spokespeople for the sector, and the real political economy meant that I wanted to understand where the field came from and was going. Hence this little book. It may not be not great, but it says everything I know about the past, present, and future of the humanities in the United States, drawing on examples from other countries as well as our own rather dubious record.

After an examination of U.S. university history and the place of the humanities within it, I look at the publishing world, since this both indexes and solidifies that place. Having established the parlous present and future of the humanities, I then address the major alternative to business as usual, breaking down the opposition with the sciences that disables our social standing to consider the pros and cons of a comprehensive turn toward the creative industries as a focal point in search of relevance, student appeal, and federal funding. I conclude by suggesting that the two humanities must merge in order to survive and thrive.

Blowup Time

*What is my place in the world as a human being preparing for a
career as an army office of the nation that stands at the forefront of
Western civilization?*
   —David Bedey, West Point professor, quoted in Carol Iannone,
    "Liberal Education at the Academy"

*In a completely free market, the humanities would clean up. Faced
with a choice between an arts degree costing £8,000 a year, and one
in science costing upwards of £30,000, history and philosophy would
suddenly become very popular.*
   —Iain Pears, "Why the Humanities Remain Highly Relevant"

*There seems to be no agreement among the students of liberal-arts
education as to the fundamental principle or principles upon which
a college curriculum ought to be built. . . . [T]here has been no
recognized integrating concept.*
   —Harvey A. Wooster, "To Unify the Liberal-Arts Curriculum"

This chapter situates the humanities within the history of U.S.
universities. That story is characterized by two tendencies: an
expansion of governmentality, in the sense of research undertaken for the public weal, teaching that trains the populace in self-
regulation, and paymasters and administrators accreting authority
over academics; and an expansion of commodification, in the sense of
research animated by corporate needs, students addressed as consumers, and collegecrats constructing themselves as corporate mimics
(Miller 2003; also see Agger and Rachlin 1983; Tuchman 2009). The
outcome has made culture an object and an agent of use, a resource
that indexes and occasions historic changes and purposive policies
(Yúdice 2003), with spectacular results for the two humanities.

Many writers within the governmentality tradition assume that it is incommensurate with Marxism, and vice versa.[1] I see no logical reason for this stance. The project of neoliberal governing-at-a-distance has its own logic and materiality, of course, but they fit the agenda and methods of corporatization as much as governmentality (Miller 2010a). Both tendencies have been at play since the emergence of higher education as part of public culture in the United States 150 years ago, and neoliberalism has heightened their influence.

The classic U.S. model of higher education aims to equip students with a liberal inclination that respects knowledge *of* a topic and *for* a purpose rather than simply knowledge *by* a particular person. The model places its faith in a discourse of professionalism, not charisma. It makes people believe in and exchange openly available knowledge as opposed to secret magic. In other words, if someone *truly* wants to know how television works as a piece of technology, or how I can write this online twenty thousand feet above Manhattan or in a Culver City bar, she is permitted access to such intelligence. She may equally subscribe to digital cable and broadband based on her confidence in the system of governmental and university research, industrial training, and accreditation that galvanizes and regulates this fraction of a culture industry. She need not do so based on the idea of electronic communication as a gift from a deity via an elect whose knowledge and power cannot be attained by others.

But the liberalism that governs knowledge has itself been transformed by the doctrine that higher education is a competitive industry and students are sovereign consumers. A radical shift in political theory is entailed in this change because it signifies that university study is not primarily about citizenship but employment. Hence it is a quasi-private, individual good, not a collective, public one. How did this state of affairs come to pass?

Despite their stature, in some ways, universities have always been the underprivileged sector of U.S. education in that they are considered inessential for the population as a whole in contrast to compulsory schooling. So unlike in the case of the primary and secondary

---

1. See, for example, special issues of *Cultural Values* (2002) and *American Behavioral Scientist* (2000).

sectors, parents and students pay major college costs directly. On the one hand, at the level of political theory, higher education is an entitlement rather than a right, so costly and valuable is it, and so jealously guarded as a site of boosterism and a route to collective prosperity and power. On the other hand, in accordance with this governing paradox, universities are *very* privileged as centers of new knowledge and investments in an uncertain future. Education and research are described as both *indices* of socioeconomic problems and *answers* to them (for example, innovative debt instruments and divisions of labor may have damned us, but structural adjustment and technological innovation will save us). Research universities suck up gigantic amounts of money based on this paradox.

Given capitalism's taste for crisis, and the currently fashionable if banally shopworn notion that this can be creative and desirable, areas such as the humanities, which maintain institutional memory of residual and discarded discourses, are expected to operate as businesses. We are told that markets should allocate university resources without cross-subsidies—provided that science and the humanities are not funded in accordance with their expenses or the number of students they attract. The humanities' "natural cost advantages"— they require minimal equipment and deliver significant enrollments at both undergraduate and graduate levels—are nullified by prices that are flattened out across the arts and sciences. Their "disadvantages"—primarily lack of access to research money—are accentuated, such that they look like "a loss-making indulgence" (Pears 2010).

Those states that compare public expenditure against student numbers and disciplines demonstrate that medicine and engineering have huge in-house costs given their enrollments when compared with, for instance, media studies (Desrochers, Lenihan, and Wellman 2010). Newfield argues that there is monumental cross-subvention on campus: the humanities subsidize science and engineering, inter alia. He calculates teaching revenues for a major public university system in ways that show the humanities well ahead of the social and natural sciences, with engineering and professional schools minor contributors, but the humanities fall drastically *behind* the sciences and engineering when it comes to generating revenue from grants and gifts, which help build buildings and pay tithes to central administration (2009: 276–77, 2010a, 2010b; also see Newfield and Barnett 2010).

It would be valuable to interrogate balance-of-payments questions internationally as well, given the vast numbers of overseas students around the world studying the humanities who pay exorbitant fees to do so (Arts and Humanities Research Council 2009). The U.K. government acknowledges such facts but responds by elevating direct state subsidies of science, technology, and medicine while requiring the humanities to charge more for classes (Independent Review of Higher Education Funding and Student Finance 2010; Gillies 2010). This is hardly surprising given the grab for managerial power and centralized authority in which market moralists merrily engage.

The reality of humanities cross-subsidies is not understood by the U.S. administrative elite, as evidenced by this telling remark on PBS from the president of the University of California system: "Many of our, if I can put it this way, businesses are in good shape. We're doing very well there. Our hospitals are full, our medical business, our medical research, the patient care. So, we have this core problem: Who is going to pay the salary of the English department? We have to have it. Who's going to pay it in sociology, in the humanities? And that's where we're running into trouble" ("College Tuition Hike" 2009). A pity there aren't more sick people, really. Perhaps we could attract them to emergency rooms by offering readings of Gloria Anzaldúa or Joseph Conrad and then ask hospitals for a capitation fee based on the uplifting qualities of literature.

So what are universities for? What is the purpose of a liberal education (arts and sciences rather than business and technology) and its subset, the humanities—and why do these things cost so much and infuriate so many? Why do these words sound so nasty?

History

In the 1830s, when the first waves of white-settler European immigration across classes began, U.S. higher education provided people and knowledge for use by the state and business and sought to integrate the population through civic culture. From the 1850s, when the country began its industrial takeoff, the emergent bourgeoisie created partnerships with tertiary education to develop a skilled workforce (Miller 2003). So our origins are highly pragmatic. Only an inaccurate—albeit lovable—account could stress "freedom of teaching" and "autonomy of research" as keynotes of this heritage (Hohendahl 2005: 3). The "subjection of the humanities to practical and commercial ends" has a long lineage (Frow 2005: 269).

Let's look more closely at this scholarly instrumentalism. Universities flowered at the turn of the twentieth century as corporations began to place more and more faith in applied science via electromagnetism, geology, chemistry, and electricity. By the 1920s, Harvard had a business school, NYU a Macy's-endorsed retail school, and Cornell a hotel school. The two World Wars provided additional pump priming and premiums on practicality from the federal government. Large research campuses actually expanded their capacity during the Depression, and the shop was comprehensively set up to cater to corporate and military research and development in the late 1950s via the Cold War. The federal government had boosted college enrollment via the Servicemen's Readjustment Act of 1944 (the GI Bill), and *Sputnik* ushered in a bipolar contest that saw monumental expansion of U.S. universities through the 1958 National Defense Education Act (Aronowitz 2000; Miller 2007c).

The shop even supported some favored quarters of humanities radicalism: Noam Chomsky's linguistic work (1965) was underwritten by the U.S. military's Joint Services Electronics Programs, and the Pentagon paid for Harold Garfinkel's foundational research into transgender identity (1992). Similar stories could be told elsewhere: Britain's Centre for Contemporary Cultural Studies began with a corporate grant (Hoggart 1973: 182–96); there is no theory of encoding by media producers versus decoding by active audiences without Italian television subsidizing Umberto Eco's research (1972); and Jean-François Lyotard's account of postmodernism (1988) emerged thanks to his consultancy for a Canadian province (Miller 1998). Despite the claim that university life involves "academic enclosure," the Research One school has long been "a vast economic enterprise" (Maniquis 1983: 135).

Ties between capital and scholarship have grown ever closer and more questionable. Corporations gave U.S. schools about $850 million in 1985, rocketing up to $4.25 billion a decade later. This development derived from the extraordinary Bayh-Dole Act of 1980, which permits nonprofit educational institutions to own and commercialize inventions, provided the state can use them as it sees fit and scholars do not hold patents derived from federally financed research. Before the act, research schools collectively accounted for about 250 patents per year. Now, the figure is close to 5,000. In 1999, the top hundred universities received $641 million in royalties, up by almost $500 million in just four years. Patent applications filed in the major centers—the United States, Japan, and Western Europe—increased by 40 percent between 1992 and 2002, to 850,000 per year (Donoghue 2010; Poovey 2001; Newfield 2003, 2004, 2008; Organisation for Economic Co-operation and Development 2004).

Along the way, governmentalization and commodification have merged in their concerns and methods. So the multinational pharmaceutical corporation Novartis funded more than a third of the activities of the Plant Biology Department at the University of California, Berkeley, between 1998 and 2003. A faculty member who criticized this arrangement was denied tenure—a decision that external reviewers found was influenced by the prevailing political economy (Busch et al. 2004). And the Massachusetts Institute of Technology (MIT) media laboratory is a playpen provided by corporations for apolitical graduate students working with implicit and explicit theories of possessive individualism—an ethos of fun in which the latter may privately claim to be subverting their paymasters but do so in ways that are eerily reminiscent of the dot-com boom's empty cybertarianism:

The Lab's primary source of funding comes from more than 60 corporate sponsors whose businesses range from electronics to entertainment, furniture to finance, and toys to telecommunications. Sponsorship is available in several different options . . . [and] provides a unique opportunity for corporations to have access to a valuable resource for conducting research that is too costly or too "far out" to be accommodated within a corporate environment. It is also an opportunity for corporations to bring their business challenges and concerns to the Lab to see the solutions our researchers present. (MIT Media Lab, n.d.)

Industrial research parks characterize such schools as Texas, Massachusetts, Duke, North Carolina, and Stanford. The NSF established dozens of engineering research centers in the 1980s with the expectation of "partnerships" flowering between corporations and higher education that function as public welfare for "entrepreneurs" (Rhoades and Slaughter 1998: 36). Meanwhile, the public interest has been compromised by amendments to state laws throughout the country that have quietly exempted publicly funded scientists from conflict-of-interest responsibilities that apply to refuse workers or personnel officers.

The notion of partnerships applies to teaching as well as research. The National Governors Association (NGA) has decreed that increasing student participation and completion must couple "academic success" to "the needs of the marketplace" through labor-market planning and state and capital participation in curriculum. This is described as "external awareness" in contrast to what are derided as "internal customs" (Sparks and Waits 2011: 2–3, 5, 11). Academic freedom, the nature of research, and theories of citizenship are as lacking from this divination as scholarly rigor and educational research: The association's "study" on the topic cites web addresses, official reports, and little else.

We can see another corporate tendency: transferring the cost of running schools away from governments and toward students, who are increasingly regarded as customers investing in human capital. And what investments they are. Since 1980, the consumer price index has gone up 179 percent, but college tuition has increased 827 percent. What used to cost a quarter of middle-class family income each year now accounts for well over half (Henwood 2010; Newfield 2003, 2008). How quaint that Bruce Johnstone, a former chancellor of the State University of New York, rejoiced that students "assume greater personal responsibility for their learning" (quoted in Martin 1998: 9).

According to the coin-operated right-wing think tanks that set up their stall against secular higher education, the reasons are that government subsidies have made it easy for universities to raise prices and faculty salaries have increased. Consider this parody of the position: "Plushy professors, drunk on self-satisfaction, sprawl on satin couches, stomachs poking upward, while their half-naked students stagger out the back door to a lifetime of rag-picking" (Grafton 2010). This explanation is part of the reflexive reaction from pundits-for-hire whenever democracies respond to voters' wishes. It is empirically false: Pay for full-time professors since the early 1990s is just a wee bit ahead of inflation, and precarious sessional teaching has become a norm, as we have seen (Deresiewicz 2011).

The truth lies in two facts. First, fancy private universities are splurging on saunas, supercolliders, and screens (TVs, computers, phones, and tablets) in order to attract top students. Second, in the case of public schools, there have been massive declines in state funding. In 1980–1981, the three levels of government accounted for 48.3 percent of their income, whereas the proportion was 38 percent in 1995–1996. Tertiary education's overall proportion of public appropriations declined from 6.7 percent to 4.5 percent between 1975 and 2000. By 2005, state investment in public university students was at its lowest level in a quarter of a century, and public revenues increased by just 6 percent as a proportion of college finances during 1998–2008, despite vastly greater student numbers (but don't worry; expenditure on college "football" per student-athlete roared upward). Tuition paid for 38 percent of the cost of public schools in 1998 and more than 50 percent in 2008, a trend that doubled student debt between 1992 and 2000 and again over the next decade. At the end of 2011, it stood at a trillion dollars. Meanwhile, a record 9.1 percent of recent graduates were unemployed in 2010 (Newfield 2008, 2009; Henwood 2010; Miller 2007c; Martin 2009; Desrochers, Lenihan, and Wellman 2010; Project on Student Debt 2011).

A dual faculty-student financial dependence on private sources is twinned with the mimetic managerial fallacy, a process whereby governments and university administrators construct corporate life as their desired other. This is part of "the business revolution" in which "codes of business judgment have presented themselves as universal knowledge" (Bruno and Newfield 2010). Universities are increasingly prone to puerile managerial warlockcraft superstitions about "excellence," "quality control," and "flatter structures" (I guess the latter refers to a California parking lot after an earthquake). In addition, academic institutions have come to resemble the entities they now serve as colleges are transformed into big businesses/government secretariats. Major research schools, particularly private ones, are also landlords, tax havens, and research-and-development surrogates whose trustees look for returns on collective and individual investments (Giroux 2007; Giroux and Myrsiades 2001).

One can find instances of the mimetic managerial fallacy in any university administration, but it is hard to go past one collegecrat informing the *New York Times Magazine* that "being president of the University of California is like being manager of a cemetery: there are many people under you, but no one is listening. I listen to them" (Solomon 2009). But he is not really alone, this poor pseudo-isolate: His seemingly solitary life at the top is actually quite sociable, because the mimetic fallacy has seen nonteaching managers increase their proportion from a tenth to a fifth of employees across U.S. schools in the last three decades. The upshot of such ecstatically parthenogenetic managerialism is that more and more senior and junior administrative positions are created. Universities have added so many managers (a 240 percent increase from 1976 to 2001) that faculty amount to just a third of campus workers. And whereas senior faculty members are frequently replaced by assistant professors or adjuncts, senior managers tend to be replaced by those of equivalent rank (Deresiewicz 2011; Martin 2011). Reach out and feel the love. Apparatchiks are just a coquettish glance away.

Consider the Chancellor Who Came In from the Cold thanks to the reality television show *Undercover Boss* (2010–) on CBS, which was nominated for an Emmy as "Outstanding Reality Program" in 2010 and 2011 ("Undercover Boss" 2012). It follows corporate executives as they venture incognito into factories to experience grassroots life in their companies. To me, this smacks of unreconstructed Maoism. It's rather reminiscent of Deng Xiaoping being sent off to the Xinjian County Tractor Factory during the Cultural Revolution for some political reeducation courtesy of participant observation of the working class (Wang 2003).

But no. Part of the wider reality-television phenomenon, *Undercover Boss* is a banal example of game shows taken into the community, *cinéma vérité* conceits, scripts written in postproduction, and *ethoi* of Social Darwinism, surveillance, and gossip. Makeover shows like this one target economically underprivileged viewers, offering them a lifestyle they cannot afford to sustain. The genre emphasizes the responsibility of people to master their drives and harness their energies to secure better jobs, homes, looks, and lovers. It is suffused with deregulatory *nostra* of individual responsibility, avarice, possessive individualism, hypercompetitiveness, and commodification.

The chancellor of the University of California, Riverside (UCR), appeared on *Undercover Boss* in 2011. In typical gringo fashion (though he is originally from Argentina), the show began and ended in tears. The chancellor cried about personal loss. He cried about student debt. He almost cried about putting in false teeth and wearing a Groucho mustache as part of his thrilling disguise. He looked miserable as he tried to function as an athletic coach, a library assistant, a science adjunct—you name it.

But then he removed the disguise and came out, out of the closet of the faux proletariat. And his young mentors in these various failed real jobs were rewarded. Student loans? Forgiven. Poor athletic facilities? Sorted (a promise of $2 million for capital improvements). Untenured junior faculty? Supported. It was magic, provided by unnamed benefactors.

What an absurd moment—but as Socratic folks like to say, a teachable one. It cloaked the horrors of a system that puts children of the working class into generational debt and wastes millions of dollars on anti-educational sports programs. The cloak was one-off charity, made available to those lucky enough to be subject to childish deceit by a media corporation and a public servant. What was going on here, at a time when "his" campus had to cut $37 million from its budget—a figure that had the potential to double by the end of that northern summer—but was "investing" $10 million in a medical school?

Reality television humanizes managers. It gives workers a get-out-of-debt card. It brought UCR's chancellor down to earth by allowing him to construct universities in an hour of prime-time mass TV as teaching institutions where the humanities do not exist. Go CBS. Go UCR. Go *Undercover Boss*. We love and honor you.

The mimetic managerial fallacy also stimulates surveillance. Regional accrediting institutions that vouch for the quality of U.S. degrees have been in place for well over a century. But since the 1970s, there have been vast increases in auditing work: from outside the university, on the campus itself, within departments, and in how faculty members view themselves. For example, we have seen ever-increasing performance-based evaluations of teaching at departmental and decanal levels rather than in terms of the standard of an overall school. Such methods are used by 95 percent of departments (for the impact on feminist professors and faculty of color, see Valdivia 2001).

Grants and commodification are valorized over publication, and administrators refer to "change" as an unproblematic good that they adore and admire. This means more obedience, more external review, more metrification of tasks, more forms, less autonomy, and less time to research. "Change" refers, really, to managerial mistrust of academics. It is a new kind of conformity, to national and international governmentalization and commodification in which faculty devote vast amounts of time to filling out forms describing what they have done, are doing, and intend to do and a new class of unaccountable evaluators has mushroomed to police us. The picture is starkly sketched in Gaye Tuchman's ethnography *Wannabe U* (2009).

Administrators frequently link budgets to outcomes, in keeping with the prevailing beliefs of public-policy mandarins—their restless quest to conduct themselves like captains of industry. As successive superstitions come along—the 1990s variety was Total Quality Management—administrators fall in line with beguiling *doxa*. Along the way, faculty-student ratios worsen, and reporting, surveillance, and administration grow in size and power (Miller 2009c). Many of us who have actually worked for business, the military, or government know what laughably inefficient institutions they can be—but folks who watch academics research and teach from the perch of administration frequently have ressentiment in their eyes and underachievement on their résumés, kicking down even as they kiss up. We are told to do more with less. It's all rather reminiscent of an erectile-dysfunction promotion.

The result is a significant realignment of power. Shifting the burden onto students to pay for their education supposedly makes them keener learners, while encouraging additional scrutiny of the classroom is said to transform a space of traditionally unequal power relations. But that Pollyannaish analysis will not do. First, as more and more funding comes from private sources, corporations crave returns on their investments, both ideologically and monetarily. Second, the address of students as liberal agents both distorts their actual subject-positions and underprepares them for the obedience and absence of free speech required in most workplaces, in addition to adding to the central power of has-been and never-were academic administrators over working scholars. Of course, there are contradictions here as well. As Ross (2010) has shown, the contemporary university is split between *l'art pour l'art*, the desire for profit, and the need to obey the state. Sometimes these forms of life coexist harmoniously; sometimes they don't. But I think the balance is shifting decisively.

The Humanities

Having considered the macrocontext, it is appropriate now to examine the history of the humanities within it. What *are* they?

Some very restricted accounts limit the definition to researching and teaching "literary, philosophical and historical texts" (Fish 2008a) with a remit "to evaluate the past, not invent the future" (Bauerlein 2008). The bias toward literary criticism in such definitions is particularly strong. The American Council of Learned Societies (ACLS), for example, which represents dozens of professional associations with memberships between 500 and 150,000 (Yu 2008), describes the high priest of criticism Matthew Arnold as a "great Victorian spokesman for humanities and culture" (Levine et al. 1989: 1). The Mellon Foundation, probably the nation's biggest funder of the sector at upward of $200 million a year, privileges "history, literature, and philosophy" and extramural cultural institutions (Ekman 1995; Yu 2008; see also http://www.mellon.org). In 1965, Congress listed the following humanities fields: archaeology, comparative religion, ethics, history, languages and linguistics, literature, jurisprudence, philosophy, and history, theory, and criticism of the arts (Gillies 2010). Today's *New York Times* defines the humanities as "languages, literature, the arts, history, cultural studies, philosophy and religion" (P. Cohen, 2009).

These accounts clearly privilege Humanities One, a form of life that is tenuous in the Humanities Two of big public universities, especially non–Research One doctoral institutions, in comparison with communication and media studies.

Arnold's recipe for criticism elevated it over other forms of knowledge as a focus on *"the best that is known and thought in the world"* (1875: 45). This implied both a disciplined approach to the materiality of texts—what they say—along with a concern for the forms of life they represent (Hall 2004). The ACLS has recognized that its mission must be wider than the world imagined by littérateurs, so it encompasses "the foundations of aesthetic, ethical, and cultural values," which expressly include anthropology, psychology, and sociology (American Council of Learned Societies 2012). When I sit on ACLS review bodies, we consider applicants for funding from political science as well as classics.

And elsewhere, the distinction between Humanities One and Two is very blurred. In Australia, the Council for the Humanities, Arts and Social Sciences (2012) specifies "philosophy[,] languages, literature studies and history, and anthropology." The Netherlands Committee on the National Plan for the Future of the Humanities nominates "languages and cultures, literature and the arts, history and archaeology, religions, ethics, gender and philosophy . . . communication and media studies" (2009: 11). In the U.K., the Arts and Humanities Research Council (AHRC; 2009) identifies "history, classics, archaeology, English literature, philosophy, religion, law, modern languages, linguistics, informatics, media studies, drama, music and design."

The European Commission avows that the humanities

are adapting to a new context characterized by rapid internationalisation and new demands emanating from new clients. This shift away from national canons has however predated contemporary calls for international collaborations in humanities research: starting in the 1970s, various movements in philosophy, literature and history have questioned the legitimacy of such canons and their collusion with certain forms and distributions of power. These important developments led to considerable disciplinary renewal. They facilitated the

questioning of the distinctions between "high" and "low" culture and the engagement of the humanities with popular culture, and the development of new and important fields, such as
media studies. They displaced national frames of cultural self-
understanding and questioned them in ways that destabilised
the centrality of the modern enlightened subject. (2009: 19)

Some expansive humanities institutes in the United States include
"traditional humanities departments; crosscutting work in such interdisciplinary areas as ethnic studies, gender studies and new con-
figurations in area studies or global studies; all aspects of the arts as
well as narrative or theoretical social sciences; policy studies; legal
theory; and science, technology, and information studies" (Davidson
and Goldberg 2004: 43).

The humanities have a complex prehistory that helps explain this
capacious, even capricious nature, as incarnated in latter-day gringo
fetishes. Their genealogy begins with the formation of elite masculinity in ancient Athens and Rome, when carefully modulated desire
could be a sign of fitness to govern others through a judicious but
pleasurable mixture of austerity and hedonism. According to the key
authors of that tradition, the male body was the locus for an ethics
of the self, a combat with pleasure and pain that enabled future leaders to know the truth by mastering themselves in a series of tests and
doubts that became mantras for modern-day classics and ancient philosophy. Xenophon, Socrates, and Diogenes believed that decadence
led to professional failure unless it was accompanied by regular examination of the conscience and physical training, while Aristotle
and Plato favored regular flirtations with excess, tempered by discipline (Foucault 1986b: 66–69, 72–73, 104, 120, 197–98). For Solon, the
key task of any ruler was "to check the desires that are excessive" and
"make crooked judgments straight" (1994: 39). Self-control and physical power were part of studying to lead: Plato's very name referenced
the width of his martial shoulders, which continue to inspire pop phi-
losophers' love of combat (D. Young 2010).

Five hundred years "after" Athens, the sexual ethics of ancient
Rome saw spirituality emerge to enrich material exercises of the self
as training for governance

within an ethics that posits that death, disease, [and] even physical suffering do not constitute true ills and that it is better to take pains over one's soul than to devote one's care to the maintenance of the body. But in fact the focus of attention in these practices of the self is the point where the ills of the body and those of the soul can communicate with one another and exchange their distresses; where the bad habits of the soul can entail physical miseries, while the excesses of the body manifest and maintain the failings of the soul. (Foucault 1988: 56–57)

In addition to the excesses that preoccupied fourth-century B.C. Athens, first-century A.D. Rome was concerned with physical frailty: the finitude of life and fitness. Moral arguments were imbued with "nature and reason," joining exercises of the self to more elevated quests for truth (Foucault 1988: 238–39).

This tradition of leadership through self-control continued with other thinkers who became sages of the U.S. curriculum, especially Humanities One. Augustine explained Adam and Eve's postapple physical shame as a problem of control: Sexual organs that were easily managed before the Fall suddenly became liable to "a novel disturbance in their disobedient flesh" because Adam had disobeyed God. That left the rest of us with original sin. The pudenda, or "parts of shame," were named as such because lust could "arouse those members independently of decision." The "movements of their body" manifested "indecent novelty" and hence shame because the "genital organs have become as it were the private property of lust" (Augustine 1976: 522–23, 578, 581). Such feelings derived from the capacity of desire to get out of whack. As Foucault put it, what were once "like the fingers" in obeying the will of their owner came to elude his control, a punishment for Adam's attempt to evade God's will (Foucault and Sennett 1982; also see Porter 1991: 206).

Only law and leadership could restore that self-control, or at least mimic it, by channeling hypermasculinity in the interest of social order and imperial expansion. Enter the humanities *avant la lettre* and their later advent in liberal U.S. education as instruments of governance and commodification—once "culture" had emerged as a concept.

The word *culture* derives from the Latin *colere*, which implied tending and developing agriculture as part of subsistence (Adorno 2009: 146). With the advent of capitalism's division of labor, culture came both to *embody* instrumentalism and to *abjure* it, via the industrialization of farming, on the one hand, and the cultivation of individual taste, on the other. Eighteenth-century German, French, and Spanish dictionaries bear witness to a metaphorical shift from agricultural cultivation to spiritual elevation. As the spread of literacy and printing saw customs and laws passed on, governed, and adjudicated through the written word, cultural texts supplemented and supplanted physical force as guarantors of authority. With the Industrial Revolution, populations urbanized, food was imported, textual forms were exchanged, and consumer society produced horse racing, opera, art exhibits, masquerades, and balls. The impact of this shift was indexed in cultural labor: *poligrafi* in fifteenth-century Venice and hacks in eighteenth-century London wrote popular and influential conduct books. These works of instruction on everyday life marked the textualization of custom and the appearance of new occupational identities. Anxieties about "cultural invasion" also date from this period, via Islamic debates over Western domination. The humanities emerged as secular alternatives to deistic knowledge (Miller 2009a; Schelling 1914: 180) focused on *"self-realization"* (Weber 2000), per the classical tradition outlined previously, redisposed to account for the emergence of the modern sovereign state and nationalism.

Immanuel Kant's *Critique of Judgment* was a crucial contribution to ideologizing these shifts. He argued that culture ensured "conformity to law without a law." Universities must use aesthetics to generate "morally practical precepts," schooling people to transcend particular interests via the development of a *"public* sense, *i.e.* a critical faculty which in its reflective act takes account (*a priori*) of the mode of representation . . . to weight its judgement with the collective reason of mankind" (1952: 86, 10, 151; also see Hunter 2008: 590). Kant's *Political Writings* envisage an *"emergence from . . . self-incurred immaturity"* that is independent of religious, governmental, or commercial direction and animated by the desire to lead rather than consume (1991: 54). For Samuel Taylor Coleridge, "The fountain heads of the humanities" are "watching over" the sciences, "cultivating and enlarging the knowledge already possessed" because "we must be men in order to be citizens" (1839: 46).

This relates to the origins of the humanities, for it has long been argued that creating one's own stories rather than importing them is crucial to civic culture. So Herman Melville opposed the nineteenth-century U.S. literary and educational establishments' devotion to all things English as an obstacle to bringing "Republicanism into literature" (Newcomb 1996: 94). Ironically, such self-reliance meant morality was no longer absolute. Rather, it was the outcome of applied reasoning based on each person's ethical substance through a dialectical struggle with desire, constraint, individuality, and collectivity. While the distinctively human capacity for intellection was laden with moral purpose, it was indissoluble from the craven desires that simply came from being alive and an inevitably mediated access to knowledge. The two modulated each other, with principle and pleasure in constant combat. Virtue derived not from resolving the conflict, which was impossible, but from governing it wisely (McHoul and Rapley 2001: 439–40).

Although many have queried the expansion of Kant's ideas beyond visual art and into literature and history, his impact has been to expand the purview and claims of the humanities (Rorty 1994: 578). In imperial Britain, for example, the humanities formed "the core of the educational system and were believed to have peculiar virtues in producing politicians, civil servants, Imperial administrators and legislators" because they incarnated and indexed "the arcane wisdom of the Establishment" (Plumb 1964: 7)—what Arnold called "that powerful but at present somewhat narrow-toned organ, the modern Englishman" (1875: x). A century ago, U.S. universities were dominated in their turn by moral philosophy, Latin, and Greek (Ayers 2009: 25) in an attempt to match and transcend the "narrow-toned organ."

Then "the rising tide of scientific and industrial societies, combined with the battering of two World Wars . . . shattered the confidence of humanists in their capacity to lead" (Plumb 1964: 7). Over the past century, the various classical and classics associations in the United States showed considerable anxiety about the role of the humanities in such developments and their place in it. I focus on some relevant remarks from their metacritiques. These Olympian pronouncements do not describe the totality of classics in terms of pedagogy or research in either the past or the present, but the consistency of their position as synoptic statements across decades is remarkable (Thomas Scanlon, pers. comm., 2011). They indicate that Humanities One has long been unstable in its composition and self-assurance.

Felix E. Schelling told a Columbia fraternity in 1913 that the "humanities, the liberal arts" were "very impractical and very desirable to possess . . . redolent of times long gone and smacking of generations before the last" by contrast with "glittering, new-minted epithets like 'sociology' [and] 'equal suffrage'" that spoke to "the life-sapping blight of hand-to-mouth utilitarianism." At the same time, the humanities were seen to produce the chivalrous and martial masculinity required of leadership, a means of making "each full-grown male into a miniature steel fortress . . . cherishing his honor, his lady and his life." The Kantian notion of developing taste was deemed crucial to "the mental and aesthetic cultivation most properly befitting a man": to be a "passionate lover" and "paragon of social and political graces" as opposed to "a submissive follower in the wake of a degenerating public opinion." The humanities and the natural sciences were higher forms of knowledge, thanks to an "elevated spirit of disinterestedness" that rejected commodified views of life (1914: 179–83). The epitome of these qualities in Schelling's eyes was Sir Philip Sydney (notable, inter alia, for extremely pragmatic work as a diplomat and for justifying his father's brutal imperial control of Ireland. Let's not focus on such matters. Why spoil a good myth?). And Schelling was rhapsodizing a curriculum in decline. Yale and Harvard removed Greek as a requirement in the late nineteenth century, which changed the aptitudes and interests of students quite dramatically—98 percent of the Yale entering class of 1907 could read the language, but that number had halved by 1921, when just 8 percent studied it in college (Donoghue 2010).

Schelling's 1939 equivalent was Howard F. Lowry. Speaking to the Ohio Classical Conference, he juxtaposed "the old and the new humanities" and the necessity to confront a "world where time and space would be but the flick of a finger, where man himself would be only the rushing, driving automaton in a 'stream-lined' land of tomorrow." In true Kantian fashion, the "best self contends against" the "ordinary self." The humanities had civilized base needs, distinguishing people from animals. But this function of the "old humanities" was compromised by "a merely contemporary and pragmatic attainment of man's best self," which was supplanting "mellowed men and women whose culture is the culture of the years" (Lowry 1941: 197, 199–200).

Lowry was referring to the displacement of classics as a privileged entry point into civilization. Thirty years earlier, the threat had come from the social and applied sciences. Now it came from a triumphantly acquisitive near neighbor: English was making a play for the mantle of entrée to civilization. Before World War I, critiques had emerged that teaching texts to school pupils that were distant from their experience of life produced rote learning and "insincerity of response," whereas English could use everyday artifacts to stimulate participation (Hunter 1996).

Lowry feared that "English has run away with the game." Removing Latin and Greek as college entry requirements was a "crime . . . committed against American youth" to the point where "many college men and women cannot even read" for want of "a good knuckle-breaking course in parsing." All "eminent English writers" had attained that status without studying English or taking classes in "how to write a poem or a play in ten easy lessons." Instead, they benefited from a classical training, which wisely focused on "self-reform" over "social-reform," thereby aiding in the creation of "a race of men who are *worth* the saving" (Lowry 1941: 202–4, 207). Such language drew on Arnold's idea of "*disinterestedness*," by which he meant "keeping aloof from what is called 'the practical view of things'" as an antidote to utilitarianism (1875: 21). This was valued for its "detachment from affairs of the present" in favor of "contemplation of the values of the past" (Wooster 1932: 373).

Three decades on from these muscular yet spiritual accounts of the U.S. humanities, written on the cusp of World Wars I and II respectively, came Gerald F. Else's mid–Viet Nam War version. His title troped Lowry's: "The Old and the New Humanities." Else was concerned that the displacement of the classics from the center of the humanities curriculum had diminished the country's ability "to develop educated taste" through an impact on language and the capacity to judge and persuade, thereby compromising the creation of "*the whole man* . . . a moral person and a responsible citizen or political leader" (1969: 803).

Like his predecessors, Else argued that the ultimate goal of universities should be to emulate the Athenian and Roman authors adumbrated previously and "civilize a passel of barbarians through and in the use of language." Even though Latin and Greek were no longer in ordinary use, they afforded the means to do this thanks to the "stylistic virtue" of their canonical works, which held an enduringly "great aesthetic appeal (as well as high moral-political quality)" (1969: 803).

The indivisibility of politics, morality, and style ramified the martial ideas of the humanities still further, with "beauty . . . the enticement to the whole operation." The rot set in when a doctrine of equivalence saw all forms of communication accorded this task—when different languages and literatures were given equal value. This shattered the unity ensured by a focus on Athens and Rome, displacing "excellent" with "representative" as a criterion for canonical inclusion. A new "diversity" meant that "educated men . . . from Italy to Iceland" no longer shared the same background derived from caste training and hence lacked a common form of "reasoning and persuasion," such that the independent use of "logical and rhetorical" forms had no collective base. Classics offered particular insights into "moral-political issues," not just pleasure, delving into "the best definition of the duties of man in society, man responsible for his society, man guiding the destinies of his society." The debaters and authors who constructed the U.S. Constitution allegedly personified the timeless value of Athenian and Roman political theory and remorselessly cited it as guidance. The failure of the modern humanities was to emphasize "the average—that is, the private—person" rather than "the future ruler or active citizen," whose pastoral and analytic development had been ceded to the social sciences. The art of "reasoned persuasion" had migrated to "the professionals of Madison Avenue" (Else 1969: 804–7).

Despite this antediluvian gloom, decades later there are no fewer than six academic societies focused on "Greek and Roman studies" in the United States (O'Donnell 2010: 47–48).[2] And as Thomas Scanlon says, "The ethos of the military male is certainly part of this humanistic inheritance, not least in the term 'virtue,' Latin *virtus*, which

---

2. I do not suggest that they still forward a martial agenda.

means 'virile courage,' especially on the battlefield. The Greek word for courage is *andreia*, again 'manly valor.' Renaissance Europeans loved this and so did the Third Reich. The Latin tattoos on the arms of US Special Services militias carry on the cachet of *virtus*" (pers. comm., 2011). The martial mission of the humanities has continued, regardless of classics' overall condition. Military professors interpret *Platoon* (Oliver Stone, 1986) and *Full Metal Jacket* (Stanley Kubrick, 1987) as tales of an "Everyman who prevails against both a sadistic trainer and the enemy in combat." Coast Guard Auxiliary cadets venture to Florence, sketching plaster casts in order to broaden their worldview. West Point cultivates its charges through summer immersion in different nations and languages—450 of them across fifty countries in 2009—and gets people to dress up and speak "Farsi and Dari" each year to mimic the experience of invading the other (Flammang 2007; Keith 2010). Maryland's Naval Academy "provides a top liberal education to all midshipmen" to ensure they understand "global and cross-cultural dynamics." This is in keeping with the navy and marine corps' *Cooperative Strategy for Twenty-First Century Seapower*, which requires students to study "Western Civilization I" and "Western Civilization II" along with classes on Asia and the Middle East (Yu, Disher, and Phillips 2010).

For West Point physics academic David Bedey, "The education of the future leaders of our Army" must emphasize "a 'long war' against radical Islam" via "an intangible—almost mystical—ethos: 'Duty, Honor, Country'" to manufacture "the best army in the world." The humanities are part of a core curriculum that can achieve this aim (alongside more instrumental subjects) by requiring cadets to interrogate their subjectivity and stand for "*Western civilization*" by querying, inter alia, one's interiority while remaining certain of "the value of one's own culture." This can be achieved through the "study of Western civilization and its American manifestation," thereby "making clear what it is we must fight for": to "counter the Islamists" with "over two thousand years of evolving Western civilization" in contrast to that "barbaric belief system" (Iannone 2008: 90). On retirement, Bedey (2008) argued that the left's influence on liberal education necessitated a "battle for the very soul of our nation. . . . [S]ilence equals appeasement." As I write these words, I am wearing a red T-shirt with images of Marxism on it. That makes me irrelevant to such debates. For the Western Enlightenment personified in Marx and Engels is not the one being spoken about.

The Air Force Academy loves the traditional humanities, delivered in a mode of hierarchical servility. It requires students to "wear uniforms, come to attention at the beginning of each session, and liberally sprinkle the words 'sir' and 'ma'am'" (Enger, Jones, and Born 2010). This aligns with my experience teaching history to militarists, when I repeatedly stressed discomfort at their standing, saluting, and hailing me in these ways. (I also found it hard when the civilian secretary of the department derided a rather scholarly student as "a fuckin' sissy.")

Civilian graduate school is available to hundreds of military officers each year at no cost to themselves. David Petraeus (2007), director of the Central Intelligence Agency (CIA), former commander of International Security Assistance Force, commander of U.S. Forces Afghanistan, ex-commanding general of Multi-National Force—Iraq, and Princeton doctoral alum, regards this as crucial to "the development of the flexible, adaptable, creative thinkers who are so important to operations in places like Iraq and Afghanistan." He cites as an example one of his own graduate school history papers. Titled "The Invasion of Grenada: Illegal, Immoral, and the Right Thing to Do," it received an A.

In 2008, the Pentagon established the "Minerva Consortium" to articulate university research to national security (Giroux 2008). The following year, the CIA launched a Language Initiative in partnership with universities to stimulate cross-cultural competence among its bureaucrats, spies, killers, and researchers ("CIA Director" 2010). Today, defenders of the NEH proudly refer to the National Security Language Initiative as a core reason for maintaining the humanities and convene events to reassure Congress of the centrality of the humanities to "national security" in terms of values and economics (Skorton 2011; Leach 2011). No wonder Adorno remarked that "some of the most frightful hangmen National Socialism produced did not only listen to Bruckner symphonies when recovering from their abominable deeds but also understood the music" (2009: 148).

In between working for the CIA, running the Pentagon, and hectoring NATO, Eagle Scout Robert Gates was a college president in Texas. Recalling those times, he told Duke University students in 2010 about his first semester in the job, when he "had to fire a long-time football coach. I told the media at the time that I had overthrown the governments of medium-sized countries with less controversy." Very witty. Gates perorated his Durham address by asking, "Will the wise and honest here at Duke come help us do the public business of America? Because, if America's best and brightest young people will not step forward, who then can we count on to protect and sustain the greatness of this country in the 21st century?"

Literature is central to this mission. The Australian Defence Force Academy says that "students who complete a major in English will have an increased knowledge of both the Western literary heritage and their own contemporary culture. Thus, a student might read the Iliad in order to consider the ways in which concepts of heroism and leadership have changed over the centuries" (University of New South Wales 2012).

India's National Defence Academy selects English language and literature as "the medium of socialization" for its officers, whose "proficiency in the language is considered to be the hallmark of a military leader" (Gundur 2010). One can understand this in a clichéd, rather obvious, manner as colonial mimicry; as a pragmatic method of dealing with ethnically diverse languages through a lingua franca; or as a class and caste marker. It also indicates the applied nature of the humanities for militarism, because indoctrination occurs not through learning to speak and write but by interpreting the Thomases Gray and Hardy and antimilitarists like George Bernard Shaw and Joseph Heller—all via the splendidly named curriculum "English for Military Purposes" (Gundur 2010).

It could just as easily be named "English for Queer Purposes" or "English for Marxist Purposes," of course. Why? According to Foucault's classical investigations, the professor is an institutionally appointed ethical exemplar, judiciously deploying doubt and contingency as the core of interpretative pedagogy while relying on the charisma of institutional power (Hunter 1996). Humanities One adherents claim that "the capacity for critical examination of oneself and one's traditions[,] . . . real deliberation," and a universal identification with humanity derive from literature and history, apparently courtesy of a magical gestalt (Nussbaum 2009). Touchingly true believers assert this shibboleth with pulverizing frequency—and diminishing effect, absent any evidence. Lying behind much of this magic is a profoundly ideological commitment to the expressive total-ity of individualism married to a civic republicanism that denies the historically and geographically contingent apparatuses and services that guarantee its apparent timelessness (Frow 2005: 271–72). These capacities could just as easily emerge from other disciplines, such as sociology or political economy, or be questioned as desirable qualities in the first place.

Humanities One owes its modern lineage to Arnold, F. R. Leavis, and their followers—a genealogy that is much more interesting and varied than its present incarnation. Often—and wrongly—associated with establishment university politics, Leavis favored many of the same quasi-mystical concepts as his classical rivals for attention, blath-ering on about the need "to foster life" and excavate places where "real work will be done . . . energy generated . . . [and] possibility proved" because he was "avowedly concerned with the training of an *élite*." Leavis identified literature as the key center for such developments "because, properly pursued, it involves a discipline of intelligence that is at the same time a training of sensibility—of perception, qualitative response and judgement." Focusing on "the nature of thought and ex-pression" stimulated "an otherwise unattainable awareness" of "moral bearings," thereby promoting "the trained non-specialist mind" that could give the world a "coordinating consciousness." As opposed to "the specialist mind," this "Educated Man" provided a general com-pass. Leavis saw these things occurring on the margins of universities, "in the interstices of the official system," because of the "interpreta-tion of democracy which amounts to the law that no one may have anything everyone can't have" (1947: 588–89, 595, 597–99, 608), which imperiled the development of "the first-class man" (1956: 20). Leaven-ing this Olympian tone with gender and racial equality, the structural function he elaborates is close to Humanities One. But . . .

Leavis's own doctorate was in what we now call media studies: It covered the relationship of journalism and literature. Leavisites were mostly high school teachers, not professors (Hough 1964; Wright 2010). Of course, he embodied the lofty claims made for the study of modern literature from both right and left, along with the love of whining, bleating, and moaning about exclusion (though in his case, with a successful attempt to infiltrate the schools' curriculum in ways that cultural studies could only imagine).[3] But the sense of marginalization and the need to train a cadre are shared today, along with the martial heritage of charismatic leadership.

From a similarly contradictory perspective, Bloom worried during the American war in Viet Nam that the task of higher education— "to cultivate man"—was compromised by the temptation "to make the man suitable to this time or place," especially given that democracies did not encourage "disinterested love of the truth" because they associated such "honor and glory" with the dreaded "aristocracy." Democracies were presiding over "the failure of universities" because of their overweening "dedication to the useful as defined by society's demands," the influence of "a mercenary use of the mind," and "the routinization or bureaucratization of . . . radical egalitarianism" that saw "the university . . . declare a war on nature" (1974: 58–59, 63–64).

There is a cosmic ambivalence in today's oscillation between the idea of the humanities as autonomous and instrumental and of multiculturalism as part of a disinterested ethical cultivation that is also a preparation for militarism (several of my working-class students of color are quite keen on officer training). So Richard Rorty insisted that the humanities "remain indefinable and unmanageable" because their essence was change and commitment to critique. He *did*, however, define "humanistic intellectuals": people who "read books in order to enlarge their sense of what is possible and important—either for themselves or for their society." As teachers, their task was "to instill doubts in the students about the students' own self-images, and about the society to which they belong." This should be guaranteed by "academic freedom" rather than any appeal to utility (2006) even though encountering great art may "occasionally suggest to people that they must change their lives," as "romantic, starry-eyed, idealistic bookworms" are "amazed and thrilled to realize that their life could be changed by reading a book." (I assume this refers to the sequence

---

3. Ellen Seiter (2005) is, of course, a notable exception, inter alios.

in *Ferris Bueller's Day Off* [John Hughes, 1986] when teenage funsters encounter abstract expressionism in the Art Institute of Chicago and realize they are readying themselves for college.) Rorty admired the way that U.S. literary studies remained close to social movements, unlike such deracinated monocultural domains as Anglo-American philosophy. In particular, he noted that textual inclusiveness and outreach stimulated African American studies and feminism (1994: 577–78, 581). So this line sees Humanities One recognizing its shifting role in relation to demography while remaining as hidebound as ever in relation to the popular media.

For Arnoldians, of course, even that level of social engagement meant "the humanities are corrupted" because there "is hardly a trace of anything that promises *disinterested* critical inquiry" (Kermode 1997). The United Nations Educational, Scientific and Cultural Organization (UNESCO) has referred to this as "liberation from the bondage of the present" (1955: 7). There is an apparent contradiction between such a position and cultural studies' zest for popular democracy, but they share charismatic ethical exemplars and institutional locations as sources of authority. These are actually two sides of a Janus face.

Meanwhile, unsubstantiated phenomenological assertions scar most claims made for Humanities One. We are told that the sector cultivates "a sense of civic duty and citizenship . . . enabling students to assess standards of human excellence . . . [and] developing a sense of compassion" (Edelstein 2010). The president of Goucher College announces that "the future demands of citizenship will require not narrow technical or job-focused training, but rather a subtle understanding of the complex influences that shape the world we live in" (Ungar 2010). A beneficiary of University of Chicago endowed-chair law school salary scales thunders away thus: "We are in the midst of a crisis of huge proportions and grave global significance" that threatens "democratic self-government." Education is generating "useful machines, rather than complete citizens" because it neglects "the soul" (Nussbaum 2010a). There is no room here for the grubby instrumentalism of Humanities Two.

As I have written three books on citizenship explaining that it is dedicated to incompleteness rather than wholeness, I am hardly likely to show great sympathy for such rhetoric. It is poor logic and history delivered through an impressionistic Olympianism. But let's think about citizenship and the humanities anyway, since that was where I began this book.

The last two hundred years of modernity have produced three zones of citizenship, with partially overlapping but also distinct historicities. These zones are the political (conferring the right to reside and vote); the economic (the right to work and prosper); and the cultural (the right to know and speak).

They correspond to the French Revolutionary cry "liberté, égalité, fraternité" (liberty, equality, solidarity) and the Argentine left's contemporary version "ser ciudadano, tener trabajo, y ser alfabetizado" (citizenship, employment, and literacy). The first category concerns political rights; the second, material interests; and the third, cultural representations. The soul is not part of the deal.

In terms of Humanities One, we again see the claim that leaders will be developed who are superior to other people and that this will occur outside political theory (which specializes in citizenship) and education and psychology (which specialize in excellence and compassion). This is magic. And magic is generally empty rhetoric laced with heavy metaphor.

Humanities One phenomenology is indebted not only to the ancients and Kant but also to Hegel's idea of a subjectivity split by the separation of language from objects. You see the same thing in Schiller and Goethe. The separation occurs as a consequence of the division of labor or the distinction between language and reference. Ethical completeness is rent by the alienation of the economy and the distance between meaning and reality (Hunter 1988b; Miller 1993).

The alleged loss of an allegedly unified subject has provided a lodestone for the detour away from relevance within Humanities One—that circumscribed, narrow, and geographically and historically contingent thesaurus known as "theory." It privileges Freudianism, ideology critique, and other forms of expressive totality such as queer theory, ethnic studies, and deconstruction. Each relies on a dialectic that is overtly abjured but hewn to in practical terms, with the charismatic intellectual humanist an ethical exemplar of the split— but ruling—subject of the classroom.

Improbably, these true believers' seminary performances resemble nineteenth-century Protestant reading groups. In each case, a self is conjured up in engagement with a particular text and then judged by a leader whose model openness to texts is predicated on ultimate authority as the person who set the curriculum. That model subject offers the grade, sits on the doctoral committee, writes the letter of recommendation, instructs on the appropriate conferences to attend and journals to publish in, and so on—and at the same time assures students that "meaning is arbitrary" (Hunter 2006). In other words, ethical incompleteness inscribes a radical indeterminacy in the subject in the name of loyalty to a more complete entity through educational and other cultural regimens (Hunter 1988b; Miller 1993).

Half a century ago, the social anthropologist Ernest Gellner waspishly scoffed at the humanities' narcissistic equation of "humanism with being the *compleat man*" such that it alone could heal this division (1964: 63n). How much has changed today apart from the alibi, which preaches division as well as unity but continues to depend on the armature of scholastic authority and largesse?

Things must change so that we are in thrall to neither a martial masculinity that serves imperialism nor a split subjectivity that masks power. Our numbers are down in terms of tenure-track jobs, undergraduate interest, and research support. So let's reform now. Something is rotting in the state. It's past time for the Dane to linger in doubt.

The Price of Science

Monographs remain largely static objects, isolated from the interconnections of social computing, instead of being vibrant hubs for discussion and engagement.
  —Association of American University Presses Task Force,
    Sustaining Scholarly Publishing

Print academic journals are dead.
  —Thomas H. P. Gould, "The Future of Academic Publishing"

We give the copyrights of our scholarly articles and monographs to university presses, and then buy them back, or demand that our libraries buy them back, at exorbitant markups. And then no one reads them. The current tenure system obliges us all to be producers of those things, but there are no consumers.
  —Frank Donoghue, "Can the Humanities Survive the 21st
    Century?"

T his chapter takes the analysis away from grandiose historiciza-
        tion and divination to consider the mundane (and dire) state
        of humanities publishing. As the public face and record of the
sector, books and journals are dominated by Humanities One (literature and history) despite the size of Humanities Two (media and
communications) because Humanities One is located in fancy schools
with a privileged research status, which affords faculty more time
to write and greater ease to promote their ideas, especially through
books.

Publishing is the key node for discarding old and promoting new
forms of knowledge. A switching point between dominant, declin-
ing, and emergent *nostra*, it indexes power shifts in universities and
society more generally and is therefore undergoing a massive transformation. The picture I paint is one more sign that "the public isn't
being served as it should be" in the current moment (Imre Szeman,

pers. comm., 2011). The situation requires fundamental rethinking, starting with Jenine Abboushi's provocation (pers. comm., 2011) that perhaps current "academic writing in the humanities should be abandoned" because of its prolix and cloistered nature. We need to make what Nick Cohen (2011) has tellingly called "literary effort" as opposed to humanities academics' unintended message to the broader public that we "are not worth listening to or fighting for."

Humanities publishing is at a crossroads in terms of outlets, measurement, finance, and values, with lines and regulations increasingly drawn and policed elsewhere, by others, be they corporations or scientists. This necessitates a wholesale change of outlook in the context of prevailing political-economic realities.

The most important of these is that *we do not matter.* The humanities have a minor role in publishing. The money and power are located across campus. For-profit corporations recognized the potential value of science and medical journals at the onset of the Cold War because of vast amounts of freely available research and growing demand for outlets (the infamous Ján Ludvík Hoch/Robert Maxwell made his fortune in this field via Pergamon Press, paving a path for others to follow). The supply and price of academic journals boomed from the mid-1970s at the very moment economic crisis gripped the Global North. As wealthy economies turned their domestic gaze away from manufacturing and agriculture and toward services, they sought to impose restrictive intellectual-property laws on the global exchange of truth, thereby placing severe limits on how libraries could fulfill their mission of access to knowledge.

The prizes truly glitter in this arena: Annual global publishing turnover in science and medicine is estimated at $16 billion. Libraries are under pressure to invest in serials from those fields because they contain the knowledge that enables scholars to get grants and publish findings. Corporate opportunism and greed saw the price of such journals increase 200 to 300 percent *beyond the rate of inflation* between 1975 and 1995. Since that time, the development of digital technologies has seen for-profit publishers proliferate as the cost of entering the industry has diminished. Even a decade ago, an institutional subscription to a humanities journal might be less than $100, while in physics it was close to $1,500. Subscriptions for sciences journals have soared at three times the rate of their humanities counterparts. Prices have continued to outstrip inflation, although the rate slowed once libraries flexed their muscles to deal with what they term "the 'serials crisis' in scholarly publications." That signifies the price of science. Libraries today pay upward of $30,000 for annual subscriptions to many journals. Even when they come out fortnightly, that is still a corporate feast. Publishers rarely reward authors for their labor, and the latter frequently pay for the privilege of publication (Ware and Mabe 2009: 5; Alonso et al. 2003: 31; Branin and Case 1998: 475, 477; Martin 1998: 13; Givler 2002).

The average number of articles that scientists read every twelve months was 270 in 2009, up from 216 in 2003 and 150 in 1977. But they barely keep up! In 1870, just 840 articles were published on mathematics. Some 125 years later, the annual number was 50,000. Thousands of academic papers are penned each day. Scientific output doubles every five years, filling 20,000 to 25,000 peer-reviewed journals. It has been estimated that the NIH supports approximately 65,000 published papers a year (Dewatripont et al. 2006: 59; Branin and Case 1998: 476–77; Organisation for Economic Co-operation and Development 2004; Electronic Publishing Services Ltd. 2006; International Association of Scientific, Technical, and Medical Publishers 2007; Ware and Mabe 2009: 6). Two decades ago, a former director of Yale's library system put it this way: "We're drowning in information and starving for knowledge" (quoted in Branin and Case 1998: 476).

As measured by income, market share, and citations, the major corporate presses responsible for this situation are Reed Elsevier, Wiley-Blackwell, Kluwer, Taylor and Francis, and Springer (Branin and Case 1998: 475; Dewatripont et al. 2006: 5, 7, 24, 36). For-profit journals published by these private firms are created quickly and easily—there are often bounties for in-house editors who purchase them—whereas journals started by professional associations focus on quality over quantity. Impact studies indicate that the private sector goes for high-priced volume while university presses prefer low-priced excellence (Dewatripont et al. 2006: 7–8, 23, 32).

Not everyone accepts the exploitative nature of this situation. The American Mathematical Society critically surveys journal costs, despite attempts by corporate publishers to prevent its doing so through court action (undertaken around the world). And Cornell's senate calls on its members to familiarize themselves with the political economy of key journals in their fields and reject price-gouging corporations by refusing to publish with them or act as manuscript reviewers (Branin and Case 1998; Givler 2002; Cornell University Library 2005).

In addition to greed, other controversies dog these multinationals. Consider medical publishing. The pharmaceutical industry's proportion of U.S. health research grew from 13 percent in 1980 to 52 percent in 1995, and Pfizer, for example, describes academic publication as a means "to support, directly or indirectly, the marketing of our product" (quoted in Moffatt and Elliott 2007: 18). Unsurprisingly, marketing rather than science determines how to develop a new compound. The following questions are typically posed: Will a drug be declared a counter to depression or ejaculation? Which scholars will be chosen to front it and produce consensus over its benefits? And will it be announced in journal x or y? Medical education and communications companies provide ghostwriting services, paid for by corporations, that deliver material to academics and clinicians—then pay them for signing it. One in ten papers in leading medical outlets is the work of ghosts, and an astounding number of articles published in the *Journal of the American Medical Association* is attributed to people paid by pharmacorps, which pressure medical journals to print favorable research findings in return for lucrative advertising copy. The most notorious and best-documented case was Wyeth (now owned by Pfizer) promoting its deadly drug PremPro. Similarly, the tobacco industry has had a "special" relationship with *Indoor and Built Environment*, which promotes articles on tobacco in return for funding from a front organization, the International Society for the Built Environment (Miller 2008a; Fugh-Berman 2010; Young and Godlee 2007; Garne et al. 2005).

Reed Elsevier houses the important medical journal the *Lancet*.[1] For some time it also owned Spearhead Exhibitions, which organized the world's largest arms fair, Defense Systems and Equipment International. Elsevier was therefore directly involved in marketing

---

1. For those who rely on such fetishes, the *Lancet*'s impact factor and associated analities are available ("About *The Lancet*," n.d.).

and distributing weaponry. Its valued clients included noted abusers of human rights and practitioners of terrorism, militarism, and imperialism, from Syria to the United States. Cluster bombs were a specialty—and particular targets of critique in the *Lancet*. So Elsevier made huge sums from publishing disinterested medical journals that Hippocratically took as their motto "do no harm" (from Hippocrates' *Epidemics* Book I, Section XI). At the same time, the company hypocritically showcased the slogan of one of its exhibitors, the torture specialist Security Equipment Corporation: "Making grown men cry since 1975!" (see http://www.sabrered.com/servlet/StoreFront).

When this grotesquerie was pointed out by International Physicians for the Prevention of Nuclear War, Scientists for Global Responsibility, Campaign against Arms Trade, Europeans for Medical Progress, and Physicians for Social Responsibility (2005), Elsevier's hack apparatchik retorted that weapons are "central to the preservation of freedom and national security," arms fairs are better regulated than sent underground, and guns and bombs "are vital elements for life-saving activities" (Cowden 2005: 890). Presumably those would be the same activities that saw the British and U.S. governments invading Iraq and ushering in unprecedented mass killings, as uncovered in the *Lancet* (Roberts et al. 2004).

It's no surprise that a journal publishing such radical epidemiology rejected its overseers' opportunistic nonsense (The *Lancet* and the *Lancet*'s International Advisory Board 2005); that the *Journal of the Royal Society of Medicine* headlined an editorial on the topic "Reed-Elsevier's Hypocrisy in Selling Arms and Health" (Smith 2007); or that Will Self, Nick Hornby, Ian McEwan, J. M. Coetzee, A. S. Byatt, and Nadine Gordimer penned a protest note to the *Times*. Very principled people stand up against such practices, and their activism can succeed: The firm ceased its grisly involvement in mass murder (Siva 2007).[2] It's also no surprise that the humanities academy was nowhere to be seen. We had nothing to contribute.

Of course, wealthy professional associations also participate in sharp practice. For example, the American Economic Association's

---

2. I refused to review a manuscript for Elsevier at this time. When I explained my reason to the (nonmedical) editors who had requested a report, they did not reply.

journals help generate new cadres, "compliant servants of the finance industry" (Cushman 2011). Charles Ferguson's documentary *Inside Job* (2010) and associated research exposed the fact that these publishing protocols have seen leading economists opining on the public interest before, during, and after pocketing hefty sitting and speaking fees as corporate consultants and conference lounge lizards (also see Folbre 2010). These revelations prodded the sacerdotal elite to consider adopting a code of ethics to govern their cartoonish conduct and abandon the charade of double-blind reviewing, recognizing that many evaluators had financial investments in perspectives they were supporting (Berrett 2011b; Jaschik 2011). Meanwhile, even the average gringo economist was charging a hundred dollars per paper review. This is in keeping with the profession's rent-seeking *Weltanschauung*, which sees salaries rise by 3.8 percent with each article penned in a house journal (American Economic Association 2012; "What Good" 2011).

What is the background to this state of affairs? What *is* scholarly publishing?

English-language university publishing commenced with Cambridge University Press in 1584. In 1665, the Royal Society founded *Philosophical Transactions*, the first academic journal. Three years later, Oxford University Press began. U.S. university publishing started at Harvard in 1640 but lasted just fifty years, returning a century ago. The longest-standing academic publishing house in the United States is Johns Hopkins, which emerged in 1878. The next forty years saw most of today's major U.S. scholarly presses established, driven by the realization that the for-profit book market was not furthering the distribution of new knowledge (Electronic Publishing Services Ltd. 2006; Givler 2002).

Fifty years ago, the ACLS determined that "reasonably rapid publication at no expense to the author" was pretty well guaranteed across the humanities and social sciences (quoted in Alonso et al. 2003: 1). Of course, the council was referring to Humanities One yanquis writing in English, and the conjuncture was the height of Cold War subvention of research, when the growth of not-for-profit publishers matched the purchasing power of libraries.

In those days there were about sixty university presses in the United States. Now there are close to a hundred, and they publish twice as many books. The Association of Learned and Professional Society Publishers suggests that its members' backlist comprises 350,000 titles. Although university presses grew in the twentieth century, their development was uneven. Between 1920 and 1970, about one new college press started each year. But many closed, and just five opened, from 1975 to 2000, because of the cost of the space race, the American War in Viet Nam, and the oil crisis, which along with universities housing radical politics saw funding tighten. And when the Cold War ended, many remaining funding sources disappeared. In 1988, 10.4 percent of net revenue to presses came from their parent institutions. A decade later, that figure had fallen to 6.3 percent (Givler 2002).

During the halcyon years, publishers sold most of their books to libraries. Nowadays, sales are concentrated online and through megastores, with 25 percent being textbooks. Libraries account for about 20 percent of revenue. Globally, the number of books produced each year increased 45 percent between 1980 and 1990; the same period saw a net decline in their purchase by libraries. Libraries are increasingly complaining that the corporatization of scientific and medical knowledge (itself, of course, founded on public subvention) has sent subscription costs skyrocketing, with a negative effect on budgets for much cheaper but less prestigious areas. Come on down, the humanities. With the conclusion of the Cold War, libraries lost their share of overall expenditure on higher education. It stood at 2.9 percent at the dawn of the 1970s, rising to 3.5 percent in a decade. Ten years later, it had diminished to 3.1 percent. In the decade from 1986 to 1996, the largest research libraries saw monograph purchases drop by 21 percent and journal subscriptions by 7 percent, as the latter rose in price by 147 percent. The balance is shifting toward journals all the time: In 1986, these institutions bought more than thirty-two thousand books and fifteen thousand journals; in 2005, the figures were thirty thousand books and twenty-two thousand journals. Books went up in price over those two decades by 81 percent; journals, by 302 percent. The average number of monographs per student bought by libraries has dropped by over a third in the last twenty years. The top hundred or so research libraries dedicated 3.6 percent of their purchases to electronic resources in 1992–1993. By 2004–2005, the figure was 37.46 percent. Between 1997 and 2001, European libraries cut acquisitions of books and journals, even as their overall expenditure increased by 28 percent. Journals available in hard copy and online are frequently charged for twice, with the latter 90 percent of the cost of the former (though in the humanities, electronic versions are often part of physical subscriptions). Print runs of books average in the low hundreds, even given cost savings permitted by digital systems. Between 2008 and 2009, U.S. university presses saw major revenue shortfalls as hardbacks and paperbacks alike declined between 5 and 6 percent, and unit sales, close to 10 percent (American Council of Learned Societies Commission on Cyberinfrastructure for the Humanities and Social Sciences 2006: 24; Givler 2002; Branin and Case 1998: 476, 478; Alonso et al. 2003: 8; Electronic Publishing Services Ltd. 2006; Kyrillidou and Young 2006: 10–11, 21; Dewatripont et al. 2006: 17, 23; Brinkley 2009; Greco and Wharton 2010: 4). It reminds one of the Democratic Party's successful mantra from the 1992 elections—everything that should be up is down, and everything that should be down is up. What will happen in the future?

Journals

As should be clear by now, the dual tasks of certifying and disseminating knowledge under signs of the public good, the desire for inquiry, and scholarly esteem have been added to—and sometimes trumped by—the push for profit as firms charge higher and higher prices for scientific and medical journals. But they are not so comfortable today, because of academic and managerial anger at the prohibitive cost of their goods, the tendency of scientists to send out material on the web in advance of publication, and, perhaps most significantly, sections of the federal government arguing that since it funds vast amounts of this research, the results should be publicly available instanter and gratis. The state effectively pays for research many times over—through salaries, grants, and subscriptions.

Of course, digital publishing should reduce costs, enabling institutional subscribers to negotiate collectively and buy journals on a bundled, multiyear basis with guarantees about price increases and no sharp shocks. This is the preferred method for the world's biggest buyer of journals, the University of California, and major national consortia in France and Germany, though some important libraries are now buying individually, notably Harvard, Michigan, and Cornell. These oppositional tactics have also enabled a new discourse about the public good, marrying the cybertarian utopics of the technological sublime to authors' rights. Consider such twenty-first-century denunciations of the extremes of private property as the Budapest Open Access Initiative, the Berlin Declaration on Open Access to Knowledge in the Sciences and Humanities, the Organisation for Economic Co-operation and Development's Declaration on Access to Research Data from Public Funding, the Bethesda Statement on Open Access Publishing, and the work of the Union for the Public Domain, the Electronic Frontier Foundation, the World Summit on the Information Society, Creative Commons, and the Scholarly Publishing and Academic Resources Coalition. Other players include the Open Content Alliance, Latin America's Scientific Electronic Library Online, Canada's Érudit, the Japan Science and Technology Information Aggregator (Electronic), the Open Archives Initiative, the University of California's eScholarship Repository, Britain's Project Sherpa, arXiv, RePEc, DSpace, the Electronic Publishing Initiative@Columbia, and Open Access in European Networks (Dewatripont et al. 2006; Albanese 2002; Association of American University Presses Task Force 2011: 18).

The most important scholarly agencies now require funded researchers to publish in open-access journals: the Conseil Européen pour la Recherche Nucléaire (birthplace of the web), the Wellcome Trust, Britain's Research Councils, the French Centre National de la Recherche Scientifique, Germany's Max Planck Institutes, the Indian and Chinese Academies of Science, and the NIH. The NIH mandates open-access archiving for all grantees within twelve months of publication, and Wellcome does so within six (Dewatripont et al. 2006; Albanese 2002).

Of course, credulous cybertarians explain such developments as the ineffable outcome of technological change (Gould 2009 is a particularly romantic example). In fact, they are the product of purposive, collusive, and conflictual political-economic action by large and powerful institutions. The anti-Mammon manifestoes embody collective material action and democracy. In 2001, for example, 34,000 scientists from 180 countries signed a petition orchestrated by the biomedical founders of the Public Library of Science (PLoS) calling for journal articles to be available gratis online within six months of their hardcopy appearance (Dewatripont et al. 2006: 63).

Such activism is subject to severe counters from reactionary rent-seeking forces opposed to open-source knowledge. So the federal government's invaluable abstracting source, PubSCIENCE, which began in 1999 as a service to citizens seeking research on subjects of importance to them and their environments, was closed by the Republican Party in 2002 under instruction from capital in the form of the Software and Information Industry Association, which represents Elsevier and its kind (Albanese 2002). For-profit houses, operating as the International Association of Scientific, Technical, and Medical Publishers, issued the 2007 Brussels Declaration on STM [Scientific, Technical and Medical] Publishing, attacking progressive manifestoes for proposing measures that "have largely not been investigated or tested in any evidence-based manner that would pass rigorous peer review." Emboldened by this high-academic tone, the association elevated it to Jeffersonian levels, arguing that the declaration codified "principles which we believe to be self-evident." In opposition to accusations of price gouging and the utopics of open sources, it denounced non-revenue-based publishing for undermining peer review, pointed out the nature of costs incurred throughout publishing, trumpeted increased scholarly access through licensing systems, and asserted the compatibility of new knowledge and new profits. Signatories included the usual corporate suspects of academic publishing mentioned previously.

One factor weighing against open access is that not-for-profit publishers such as professional associations often sell knowledge to fund bursaries, conferences, grants, and public education, a revenue source that is imperiled by open access. But major physics journals have actually increased subscriptions since open access because they have become more prominent. The American Society for Cell Biology, which has made its journals available free online after two months since 2001 in accord with its "Position on Public Access to Scientific Literature," has not endured fiscal crisis as a consequence (American Society for Cell Biology 2007).

In 2003, PLoS started not-for profit publishing. It has become very powerful, thanks to support from cosmopolitan scholars and liberal foundations. PLoS journals publish accepted material immediately and are available through PubMedCentral, the NIH's free digital archive (Dewatripont et al. 2006: 63). Authors hold copyright over their papers, which they license, say, to BioMed Central Ltd. as open access articles under the Creative Commons Attribution License (Creative Commons, n.d.). The license permits unrestricted use, distribution, and reproduction in any medium, provided the original work is properly cited. Open access generally operates through archives or specific journals that are freely available and exempt from most copyright limitations—what PLoS calls "free availability and unrestricted use." The journals are free to read but not to generate. The idea is to cover costs through subsidy from professional associations, payment by authors (normally via an amount set aside in grants), or foundation support (Waltham 2010; Ware and Mabe 2009: 7).

I have some experience of scientific open access, having published in a medical journal under such arrangements (Sussman et al. 2006). And it all looks good, no? Our paper can be read free online. But the legal small print permitted a for-profit publication to republish the piece in a journal and book at a cost of $150 per copy without asking the authors. Then it declined to provide us with copies (Sussman et al. 2007a, 2007b).

Given the power of the sciences, perhaps the most telling outcome of this history is authorial subvention. How would that work in the humanities, where grants are meager and few and Olympian humanists denounce "journals that originated online" as "tedious and unoriginal" (Rauch 2010: 56)?

Apart from other differences between the sciences and the humanities, there is a distinction within the humanities between journals of tendency and journals of profession, as described in Table 2.1. The left-hand side is even less likely than the right to publish research derived from grants or to receive support from scholarly associations.

The left-hand side demonstrates a commitment to articulate knowledge with social change. It represents a will to link the professoriat with social movements as a primary locus of power, authorization, and responsibility. The right-hand side demonstrates a commitment

TABLE 2.1   HUMANITIES JOURNAL DISTINCTIONS

Journals of tendency	Journals of profession
Avowed political projects seeking intervention in specific time and space	Avowed truth projects seeking decontextualized, universalist knowledge
In-house manuscript reviewers arguing for and against authors' manuscripts on grounds of politics and cohesiveness	External manuscript reviewers performing double-blind reviews of manuscripts in terms of disciplinary competence and falsifiability
Open calls for manuscripts, theme issues, and responses to contemporary social questions	Access restricted to members of professional associations with lengthy periods of review and revision
Advance political positions across disciplines	Advance professional success within disciplines
Editorial collective self-selected	Editors chosen by associations
Prone to inefficiency, sudden bursts of energy and newness, and an eventual sense that the "moment" of a journal has passed	Prone to efficiency, "normal science," and a fate joined to sponsoring disciplines
Examples: *Social Text, Public Culture, Socialist Review, camera obscura, Radical History Review, History Workshop Journal, GLQ, New Left Review, Eptic, Cultural Studies*	Examples: *PMLA, Cinema Journal, Journal of Communication, American Historical Review, Journal of American History, American Literature, Communication and Critical/Cultural Studies*

to articulate knowledge with social reproduction. It represents a will to link the professoriat with universities and professions as a primary locus of power, authorization, and responsibility. One is about a transformation of the social order; the other, about its replication. Questions arise concerning how authorial subvention and hence publication through journals of tendency will work without the legitimation of professional bodies. Something may be lost. Despite the claim that people are motivated in their selection of journals in which to publish by the thought of "advancing their own careers" (Long 2010: 67), some of us are simpler folk than rent-seeking, utility-maximizing opinion leaders.

In my bumbling way, I seek three readerships for my work: scholars, the public, and stakeholders. A recent example concerns sport and sexuality. Based on an academic book I wrote some years ago (Miller 2001), I was invited to contribute an updated and abridged version to an Italian fashion-show catalogue (Miller 2006) and a queer U.S.

sports site (Miller 2007d). The latter was republished without my agreement and wrongly claimed for copyright by a general queer site (the piece was taken down, perhaps because I objected over the copyright issue). In the meantime, I had published a related op-ed piece on the subject in a fairly conservative newspaper (Miller 2007a). I was pleased that most of these things had happened, because I was reaching my intended audiences.

Then the article was republished, again without my consent, on a site that illustrated it with hard-core porn. There was no named webmaster, just a comments box. I appeared to be the text's sole author, responsible for the choice of pictures. My one recourse was to contact Google, which provided space for the site. The only way of doing so was to invoke the Digital Millennium Copyright Act (DMCA) (see http://lcWeb.loc.gov/copyright), which I dislike because it restricts the exchange of ideas. But that was the road Google required me to take. Again, the company took the site down, when I had wanted a dialogue with the webmaster.

The issues raised by this anecdote are varied. On the one hand, I endorse the Roland Barthes (1984)/Umberto Eco (1979) position that once my words have gone forward into the public sphere, they are no longer mine. I *do not* endorse the Woody Allen/Coca-Cola line, which insists on global control over products (Danan 2009; Coca-Cola Company 2012). In using the Internet and seeking a variety of audiences, I was opening myself up to appropriation. And if one engages gay-male popular-culture sites and sport over the issue of masculinity and sex, porn/erotica will clearly be a near neighbor. The dilemmas are mani*fold* and perhaps should have been mani*fest* to me *avant la lettre* (or *avant le cliché*). But they were not so obvious, and I found myself defending authorship (which I have several doubts about, other than as preventing labor exploitation) and problematizing porn (which I have few doubts about, other than as labor exploitation).

I consulted queer scholars and artists and image ethicists, who backed my decision. But the travail remains, and it reminds me of the original publication of my 2001 book. When *SportSex* was deep into production, someone asked me about the cover. I replied that I had not vetted one. But it was already visible on Amazon—a picture of a naked black man with his head cropped. Visions of Robert Mapplethorpe

rather than Umberto Eco went through my mind (see http://www
.artnet.com/ag/fulltextsearch.asp?searchstring=mapplethorpe). I com-
plained to the publisher and talked with black theorists and image-
ethics critics. On the basis of those conversations, I suggested that we
include an insert in the book of a discussion among the photographer,
the model, and me about the image. Otherwise, it would not be mentioned, and neither would the attempt to sell titles by using it. But
the publisher had bought the picture as stock footage. Authorship and
posing had been lost in the mists of commerce. So much money had
been allocated to the cover that Temple University Press ultimately
offered—and I accepted—digital blanching of the man's image to
make him look white. Hmm . . .

Books

Recently, I was puzzled by the claim I read in a footnote that William Makepeace Thackeray's *Vanity Fair* was the *fons et origo* of the
word *makeover*. Thanks to digital archiving and living librarianship,
I could search the book and find this was an error, then get the right
answer. But a small fraction of literary material, archival or otherwise, is available digitally, and much of it is subject to copyright. Had
I been seeking something from F. Scott Fitzgerald's *The Great Gatsby*,
I would have been obliged to scour a hard copy, because of the 1998
Sonny Bono Copyright Extension Act, created when Disney realized
that its copyright on Mickey Mouse was about to expire. It gave then-
senator Trent Lott money for his reelection on the very day that the
Republican congressional leader sponsored extension on copyright
of the rodent by another twenty years and expanded it to cover or-
phaned works (those without authors or legatees to claim ownership).
The outcome? About 80 percent of everything published remains
in copyright. From the same era, the DMCA jeopardizes fair use by
turning digital works into commodity forms and criminalizing their
appropriation. It is a disaster for libraries and furthers the decay of
any notion of copyright as a stimulus toward creativity (though at
least it clarifies that copyright is a subsidy for corporate indolence)
(Dewatripont et al. 2006: 9; American Council of Learned Societies
Commission on Cyberinfrastructure for the Humanities and Social
Sciences 2006: 11, 19–20; Lanchester 2007; Bromley 1999).

Meanwhile, Google trumpets a "commitment to the digital humanities," supposedly evident because it scanned twelve million volumes across four hundred languages and gave a million dollars to a dozen college research groups (this is so much?) (Orwant 2010).[3] Of course, the reality is that the company has a proprietary ownership plan—a profit-based system of knowledge that is profoundly inimical to the spirit of public libraries, on which it is allegedly founded.

So what is the future of an academic book such as *SportSex*? Some publishing houses argue that the edited collection, for example, which is frequently a site of major intellectual breakthroughs that professional associations would not support because of their review processes, is doomed. As customers now purchase online, they are thought not to embark on the serendipitous bookshop consumption of the past that led them to buy anthologies.

Meanwhile, the monograph, long a sine qua non of tenure in Humanities One, is ceasing to be viable because libraries have cut purchasing. The NEH underwrote the publication of hundreds of books from the 1970s, but the Republican Party crippled this service in the 1990s. First-time authors are now being asked to help fund production in a way that did not happen five years ago, when such a thing would have been regarded as a blight on legitimacy, a sign of vanity publishing. Presses are perceived as favoring interdisciplinary humanities work that addresses "trendy" subject matter, which is assumed to recover more costs of production than disciplinary-based writing. On the other hand, companies increasingly want monographs that can be adopted as textbooks in the mass market of Humanities Two, where repeated minor rewrites and tear-out exercise pages build in obsolescence and limit secondhand sales.[4] The private sector began a major push for the bulk of this market in 2001 when global finance capital developed an interest in textbook firms. As a consequence,

---

3. In the United States, "the digital humanities" can mean anything from cliometric analysis to ludic observation. It refers to a method of obtaining funds for conventional forms of Humanities One, dressed up in a rather straightforward electronic empiricism. So counting convicts in law reports or references to Australia in Dickens becomes worthy of grant support because it is archival and computable.
4. Rather wonderfully, the California Department of Education is required by Assembly Bill 2532 of 2002 to set maximal limits on the weight of textbooks that school pupils can be expected to lug around (California Department of Education 2011).

successful textbook sales by university presses, which once supported publication of scholarly monographs, are increasingly rare (State Public Interest Research Groups 2005; Alonso et al. 2003: 46, 7–8, 13–14, 22–23; Greco and Wharton 2010: 6–10).

In addition to financial pressures, many university presses object to the political onus of academic review being placed on their shoulders: If you get a book contract, you get tenure; if you don't, here's the pink slip. Books have become a trivially eldritch "trial by fire for job security" (Imre Szeman, pers. comm., 2011). There is the idea now of accepting manuscripts for publication but not physically printing them—they remain in lumpen digital limbo except for the few that must magically materialize to satisfy skeptical committees and adoring parents. This is a truly political-economic crisis, interlacing monetary and governmental components (Greenblatt 2002; Alonso et al. 2003: 1–2, 7, 11–12, 23, 29–30, 50; American Council of Learned Societies Commission on Cyberinfrastructure for the Humanities and Social Sciences 2006: 21).

The ACLS Commission on Cyberinfrastructure for the Humanities and Social Sciences calls for tenure procedures to acknowledge digital scholarship as a means of rewarding innovation and discouraging timidity (2006: 34). Bravo. But the academic monograph remains an excellent means of presenting extended arguments and evidence.

And people love books (Striphas 2009). In 2009, the depths of the recession, U.S. readers purchased eight hundred million volumes firsthand (McCrum 2011). Books are a stable technology. They don't shut down without electricity or as a consequence of system failure. Unless you drop them in the bath. And they operate in a universal format. By contrast, Apple, Amazon, and Google use varying e-book technologies, with limited interoperability (Association of American University Presses Task Force 2011: 8). Even within these less reliable technologies, books are on the march. They boast more iPhone applications than games, the previous market leader, while HarperCollins sells hundreds of thousands of cartridges of books for Nintendo consoles (Chatfield 2010; Lea 2010; "E-Publish or Perish" 2010; Darnton 2011; Ehrenreich 2011).

New business models are circulating in the hope of resuscitating scholarly books. The idea is to fund: authors, to subsidize production;

libraries, to purchase titles; and researchers, to proliferate reading (Dewatripont et al. 2006: 11). Many people within elite universities (not just agents of for-profit publishers) are proposing modest start-up packages for junior faculty to underwrite book publication. Scholars will be expected to join relevant professional associations, thereby strengthening not-for-profit publishing programs and underwriting quality control independent of subvention. Critics retort that publishers will make decisions on the basis of subsidy rather than merit (Alonso et al. 2003: 22–23, 27, 29–30).

Author-pays precepts are inevitably controversial, but in one sense they formalize the reality that academics provide labor free or below cost, especially as manuscript reviewers for (noneconomics) journals. Perhaps half of today's open-access science and medical journals are funded thanks to authors' payments, of between $1,000 and $3,000. These gifts (and subscriptions) are set against the average cost of $3,800 for publishing a paper in print and electronically (Ware and Mabe 2009: 7; Kaufman-Wills Group 2005: 1). That will be our future because we depend on the labor-process models of the big kids. We are the *escuincles*.

Conclusion

Hope *for* that future comes in part from the politicization of the big kids. Prominent academics have long proposed publishing in cheap science journals or pushing for increased library budgets to counter corporate greed, and many are appalled by ghost authorship undertaken on behalf of pharmaceutical overlords, inter alios.

Many journals are moving away from the cowardly pseudo-legitimacy of hiding the identities of manuscript authors and journal reviewers. And the rest of the world is shifting to measures of external impact to judge academic value: In most of Asia and parts of Europe, humanities metrics are following the logic of the sciences—what has your work done to influence others, not just fellow chorines who tick or cross it prior to acceptance? The gradual decentering of the U.S. academy as the implicit price deflator of everyone else will also see Humanities One lose its dependency on the mythology of peer review, with all the associated self-legislating dogma of professionalism

(Branin and Case 1998: 479, 481; Association of Learned and Professional Society Publishers, European Association of Science Editors, and Academy of the Learned Societies for the Social Sciences 2000; Jaschik 2011; Tötösy de Zepetnek 2010).

We should banish post facto commodification after open-source publication; follow the lead of progressives in the Elsevier and pharma controversies; support free distribution across the Global South; and resist lowest-common-denominator textbooks with endless, piddling updates designed to fleece undergraduates. Importantly, we must watch the publishing political economy of science and medicine. That will offer signs of what will happen in our tiny barrio. Understanding such tendencies may get the humanities a seat at the grown-ups' table.

More optimistically, we can rejoice in the ongoing success of books as things that people really love to write, publish, and read. Humanists who wish to write books—or fire those who do not—need to reorient themselves toward new kinds of publishing: mixed media, trade, artisanal, policy, and electronic. Above all, they must do so with the public in mind.

Creative Industries—
Credible Alternative?

Independent-minded university and college graduates from diverse
backgrounds are critical to building creative societies with innovative
foundations. [A] culture of innovation and entrepreneurship should
be promoted in all sectors of the economy, not least social agencies,
non-profit enterprises, public administration, and postsecondary and
health-care institutions.
　　—David Naylor and Stephen Toope, presidents of the Universities
　　　of Toronto and British Columbia, "Don't Swallow These
　　　Innovation Nostrums"

It is one of the great ironies of the project to challenge cultural
paternalism and celebrate audience diversity that by undermining
one bit of the ruling class, it appeared to endorse the ambitions of
another. Thus did post-Marxist academia give a progressive seal
of approval to letting the multicultural market rip; and if, as the
Austrian economist Ludwig von Mises said, the ultimate socialist
institution is the post office, then postmodernism and poststruc-
turalism have persuaded post-socialists to abandon playing post
offices and take up playing shop.
　　—David Edgar, "Playing Shops, Shopping Plays"

Creative class ideas have generated headlines like "Cities Need Gays
to Thrive" and "Be Creative or Die." They have also been slated,
attacked and written off by a mob of angry academics, wonks and
other pundits.
　　—Max Nathan, *The Wrong Stuff*

We have seen the difficulties that confront the humanities in both macro and micro ways, from enrollment to
philosophy to publication. The inevitable question set by
these provocations is what should be done? This chapter examines
an innovative answer to the crisis that recommends displacing—or

perhaps redeploying—the humanities under the sign of "creative industries," then provides a case study of its impact in the field of electronic games.

Creative-industries discourse represents the most interesting and productive response/riposte to the crisis of the humanities I have seen. Although the concept was birthed in the United States and flourishes in urban regeneration and industry policy around the world, the impact of this alternative on the scholarly humanities has been greatest elsewhere. Many gringo humanists are walled away from everyday life in comparison with their counterparts overseas. They appear unaware of these developments. But the creative-industry challenge has the potential to merge Humanities One and Two. To comprehend its trajectory, its success, and its limits, we must go back half a century to another place.

My notion of the two humanities comes from elsewhere, like everything I write. In 1956, the noted physicist and novelist C. P. Snow coined the term "Two Cultures" in Britain's soft-socialist serial the *New Statesman*. He wanted to understand separate parts of himself: "by training . . . a scientist: by vocation . . . a writer" (1987: 1). Snow expanded that 1956 column into a sizable pamphlet three years later. Its title has entered the language, along with his fine phrase "the corridors of power," which describes the work of politics and lobby groups. Snow was adept at moving between different formations in just the way that social movements, consultants, bureaucrats, and politicians must be.

Fearing that "the whole of western society is increasingly being split into two polar groups" (3), he saw the "Two Cultures" as a distinction between those who could quote the histories of Shakespeare and those who could quote the laws of thermodynamics (15)—that is, people fated to repeat the past and people destined to build the future. Snow would move from South Kensington to Greenwich Village and encounter the same artistic discourse. Each site had "about as much communication with M.I.T. as though the scientists spoke nothing but Tibetan" (2) because arts and humanities people strolled through life "as if the natural order didn't exist" (14). The "clashing point" of these discourses had the potential "to produce creative chances." Yet "very little of twentieth-century science has been assimilated into twentieth-century art" because "literary intellectuals, are natural Luddites" (16, 22).

The humanities' ressentiment at science's youthful rigor had long been evident (Wooster 1932: 374). And a year before Snow, UNESCO had presciently suggested that science's combination of "unbounded, unpredictable growth in knowledge and an objective solution to many problems . . . has dimmed the brilliance of humanistic learning" (United Nations Educational, Scientific and Cultural Organization 1955: 3).

Snow's provocation drew a banally irritated response from Leavis, whose publishers feared legal action (Snow 1987: 57) if the thermodynamic novelist read that "not only is he not a genius, he is intellectually as undistinguished as it is possible to be" (Leavis 1972). Not exactly the best that has been thought and said, old thing. Snow also attracted a sorrowful meditation from the historian J. H. Plumb, who lamented that "quips from Cicero are uncommon in the engineers' lab" and "Ahab and Jael rarely provide a parable for biologists" (1964: 7), while Ernest Gellner suggested humanists felt threatened by the idea of adding science "as one of the crucial 'cultures'" (1964: 63n). But for the littérateur Graham Hough, Snow's critique demonstrated that the humanities must embrace "a world dominated by industry and science and large organizations" or be consigned to Leavis's "never-never-land of the organic society" because of the irrelevance of disciplines that "do not make anything explode or travel faster" (1964: 96).

So half a century ago, we can see a similar discourse to the present conjuncture: a crisis for the humanities. Each one presented a stark binary of stoic independence or enthusiastic co-optation—with intense doubt being expressed about what was worth co-opting.

On the other side of the Atlantic, the economist Fritz Machlup, a neoclassical prophet of the knowledge society, was developing typologies of postindustrial work to help make the United States a research leader by focusing its efforts within a pragmatic opportunity-cost paradigm. While public intellectuals were debating the two cultures, Machlup (1958) was publishing a less-celebrated but massively influential paper, "Can There Be Too Much Research?" (1958). He went on to write *The Production and Distribution of Knowledge in the United States* (1962), a bedside essential for emerging ideologists of human capital that showed how the research-and-development emphasis of U.S. industry, state, and education was crucial to both economy and society. Machlup's book did not attain the immediate status of a classic, unlike its contemporary, Clark Kerr's *The Uses of the University* (1963), but has proven as abidingly influential as that other landmark celebration of governmentalized, commodified knowledge.

Machlup's ideas caught on with both left and right in the United States, leading to a consensus on science that only the Christianization of politics has compromised. They also provided a perennial wedge issue for the right over welfare versus creativity. Barry Goldwater, Ronald Reagan, and others were railing against "Great Society" liberalism in the mid-1960s. Their defeat in the 1964 presidential election, seemingly a death rattle for the right, was soon followed by Reagan's successful 1966 campaign for the governorship of California, which he launched with the following words: "I propose . . . 'A Creative Society' . . . to discover, enlist and mobilize the incredibly rich human resources of California [through] innumerable people of creative talent" (Reagan 1966).[1]

Reagan's rhetoric publicly birthed today's idea of using technology to unlock the creativity that is supposedly lurking, unbidden, in individuals, thereby permitting them to become happy and productive. This position has become a global lodestone of the humanities, albeit with an ironic time lag in the case of the United States because of our elite's ongoing investment in a liberal education that fetishizes culture away from science via Humanities One.

At the very moment that Snow and Leavis were testosteroning their way across the drawing room and Goldwater and Reagan were learning to love knowledge, the two-cultures binary was destabilizing: The 1950s and 1960s saw a great literary flowering of science fiction, much of it dystopic, in the wake of the technocratic nightmares of the Holocaust and atomic weaponry (Pynchon 1984). That genre indexed a developing trend.

Narratives and pictures have always had technological and business applications. But recently, relations across the cloisters have

---

1. Reagan was drawing on older ideas. In 1848, Ralph Waldo Emerson wrote that "a creative economy is the fuel of magnificence" (1909: 420).

changed, with computing technology and its applications to story-telling and art making known to people in every corner of campus. The *New York Times* refers to an "alliance of geeks and poets" (P. Cohen 2010), and collaborative mixes of the humanities and the sciences are becoming the norm in many countries (Bakhshi, Schneider, and Walker 2008: 2). This is frequently the result of deliberate policy rather than those accidents beloved of the bourgeois media's affection for happenstance over state planning (Cunningham 2006b).

As Thomas Pynchon put it, looking back on Snow's *Two Cultures* a quarter of a century after its publication, "All the cats are jumping out of the bag and even beginning to mingle. . . . The most unreconstructed of Luddites can be charmed into laying down the old sledgehammer and stroking a few keys instead" (1984: 1, 41). Today's computer scientists and engineers fetishize narrative, while textual critics and artists fetishize code. The two groups dress the same way, go to the same clubs, sleep with the same people, take the same drugs, and play the same games (Tenner 2010; Miller 2008b; for a less graphic account, see Edwards 2010). New humanists apply technologies to stories, and new scientists apply stories to technologies (Kittler 2004). This may be what Cathy N. Davidson (2008) means by "Humanities 2.0." It is certainly what Tanner Higgin (pers. comm., 2011) problematizes as "a way to gather some hard science cache[t] by showing off fancy code-skills or text-mining capability (skills that carry with them a certain privilege and thus often cut across class-based lines)." We examine those particular lines of flight later.

Snow, Machlup, and Reagan—critic, fan, and governor—were sniffing something, whether from inside or outside Pynchon's bag. The Global North soon decided that its economic future lay in finance capital and ideology rather than agriculture and manufacturing. The Global South, too, now seeks revenue from intellectual property as well as minerals and masses.

Changes in the media and associated knowledge technologies over this period are likened to a new Industrial Revolution or the Civil and Cold Wars; they are touted as a route to economic development as much as cultural and political expression. Since the 1970s, "knowledge workers" have been identified as vital to information-based industries that generate productivity gains and competitive

markets (Bar, with Simard 2006). To Cold War futurists such as former national security advisor Zbigniew Brzezinski (1969) and cultural conservative Daniel Bell (1977), converged communications and
information technologies promised the permanent removal of grubby
manufacturing from North to South and continued U.S. textual and
technical power, provided that the blandishments of socialism, and
negativity toward global business, did not create class struggle—hence
former secretary of state Henry Kissinger's consulting firm advising
that the United States must "win the battle of the world's information
flows, dominating the airwaves as Great Britain once ruled the seas"
(Rothkopf 1997: 47). The NGA suggests another side to this development: "Routine tasks that once characterized middle class work have
either been eliminated by technological change or are now conducted
by low-wage but highly skilled workers in other countries" (Sparks
and Waits 2011: 6). The Council of Graduate Schools and the Educational Testing Service suggest that "in the knowledge economy, a
graduate degree will become the new bachelor's degree, the minimal
education credential that high-skills employers require" (Stewart and
Landgraf 2010). What has this meant for the humanities?

A Road Taken

Peak bodies have started to ponder the value of Humanities Two
rather than be exclusively animated by Humanities One.[2] The National Humanities Alliance proclaims that "to survive in the increasingly knowledge-based and global economy of the 21st century,
*our businesses and citizens need information and training acquired
through humanities fields*" (2010: 4; emphasis in original). For many
academics and private and public bureaucrats, the indeterminacy en-
couraged by a multiperspectival humanities can develop citizenship
skills among the populace in handling cultural and political differences. Film schools, for instance, are simultaneously seen as uphold-
ers of an artistic tradition, gateways to industry, and contributors to
the zeitgeist. I used to work in one that fitted the second of those roles.

---

2. Peak bodies are entities that operate as spokespeople representing large groups, such
as the NEH.

Some humanities responses to economic shifts buy into individualistic fantasies of reader, audience, consumer, or player autonomy—the neoliberal intellectual's wet dream of music, movies, television, and everything else converging under the sign of empowered and creative fans, in keeping with Reagan's famous speech. This New Right of media and cultural studies invests with unparalleled zest in Schumpeterian entrepreneurs, evolutionary economics, and "creative industries." It has never seen an "app" it didn't like or a socialist idea it did. As a consequence, schools in many parts of the world are exterminating Humanities One fields in recognition that the traditional bifurcation of education versus training has broken down (Ianziti 2007), and the NGA is celebrating "innovation, imagination, and critical thinking—knowledge, that is" (Sparks and Waits 2011: 7). As per the paradoxical link between martial masculinity and multiculturalism noted previously, this desire for practical engagement has an interesting history that connects to cultural studies' Anglo origin myth.

Cultural studies began as a rejection of the high-aesthetic prejudices and pseudo-withdrawal from public life of Humanities One. Its first three decades, until the 1990s, were characterized by symbolic insurrectionism, with the progressive reader of texts and narcissographer of the self a pacific if vibrant semiotic guerrilla. The next challenge was to engage the public sphere. This represented an articulation with its own past via the foundational figure of Richard Hoggart.

Hoggart published his most famous book, *The Uses of Literacy: Aspects of Working Class Life* (1957), at the same moment as Snow's polemical pamphlet. When Hoggart testified in defense of D. H. Lawrence's *Lady Chatterley's Lover* (1961) at Penguin Books' pornography trial, the company endowed Birmingham University's Centre for Contemporary Cultural Studies, which he invented. Hoggart also became part of a tradition known in Britain as "the great and the good." It has counterparts in the United Nations' (UN) eminent persons groups, royal commissions, and collaborative bodies convened by otherwise rivalrous think tanks in the United States, for example, the American Enterprise Institute–Brookings Joint Center for Regulatory Studies. The idea is to blend popular visibility, political bipartisanship, professional expertise, and public interest in bodies that deliberate on matters of policy without the burden of party loyalty or corporate responsibility. So Hoggart served on Britain's Pilkington Committee on Broadcasting and similar inquiries into the arts, adult education, and youth services, then became a UNESCO culturecrat (Hoggart 1973: 182–96, 2005: 207).[3] His biography has inspired many others to tread the difficult path of influence as well as the facile one of critique.

Writing in that tradition, Stuart Cunningham, a distinguished theorist and historian of film and television, suggested twenty years ago that

> many people trained in cultural studies would see their primary role as being critical of the dominant political, economic and social order. When cultural theorists do turn to questions of policy, our command metaphors of resistance and opposition predispose us to view the policy making process as inevitably compromised, incomplete and inadequate, peopled with those inexpert and ungrounded in theory and history or those wielding gross forms of political power for short-term ends. (1992: 9)

He called for cultural studies to displace its "revolutionary rhetoric" with a "reformist vocation" that would draw energy and direction from "a social democratic view of citizenship and the trainings necessary to activate and motivate it" (11). This "engagement with policy" could avoid "a politics of the status quo" because cultural studies' ongoing concern with power would ground it in radicalism (11). Birmingham alum Angela McRobbie welcomed the move. She thought cultural policy offered a "missing agenda" for cultural studies, a pathway to change (1996: 335). Former policy maker and script editor Jim McGuigan also applauded, provided that the counterpublic sphere and citizenship rights were core values (2004: 21).

This policy trend within cultural studies, which in many ways picked up on Hoggart's example, took off at various sites. In late-1980s

---

3. Hoggart looks back on the Pilkington Committee as one of his proudest moments: "A proof of its force came when a wealthy man, financially interested in the establishment of commercial television, publicly burned the report in a garden bonfire, with like-minded friends in attendance" (2005: 208).

Australia, it involved both locals and scholars who had departed Thatcher's Britain, so it had strong ties to established protocols. Apart from Cunningham, key figures included Tom O'Regan, Tony Bennett, David Saunders, Ian Hunter, and Colin Mercer.[4] Their objects of analysis were the media, museums, copyright, pornography, schooling, and cultural precincts. Their methods—archival research, questionnaires, and Foucauldian theory—emphasized the foundational nature of government in the creation of the liberal individual (understood not according to U.S. politics but U.S. education, or in other words, a person open to new ideas that are delivered in a rational form and reasoned manner). In 1991, the Australian Academy of the Humanities responded to such developments, introducing its venerable members to cultural studies, cultural policy, feminism, and multiculturalism, then adding these as fellowship categories (M. Morris 2005: 111–13, 116–17).

In Latin America, similar engagements materialized in the work of Néstor García Canclini (1995) along with Rosalía Winocur Iparraguirre, Ana Rosas Mantecón, Daniel Mato, Ana Maria Ochoa Gautier, Bianca Freire, Alejandro Grimson, João Freire Filho, and Eduardo Nivón. In Britain, cognate practice was under way at the Greater London Council (Lewis 1983, 1985, 1986, 1991). In Canada, policy has never been far from the concerns of a people who are uniquely placed to value and criticize cultural imperialism and its nationalistic counters and who inherit a rich blend of economic and textual analysis. These qualities are evident in the work of such figures as Will Straw, Rebecca Sullivan, Jody Berland, Ric Gruneau, Charles Acland, Paul Attalah, Michael Dorland, Clive Robertson, Bart Beaty, Ron Burnett, David Taras, Ira Wagman, Vincent Mosco, Serra Tinic, Yuezhi Zhao, and Catherine McKercher.

Many prominent figures in U.S. cultural studies were similarly dubious about safely sidelined critique. They were either supportive of these developments or autonomously involved in equivalent tendencies. A quick list would feature James Carey, Manju Pendakur, Larry Grossberg, Andrew Ross, Bill Grantham, Paula Chakravartty,

---

4. I worked with them in the two cities where the tendency took firmest hold, Brisbane and Perth.

Jennifer Holt, Fred Myers, George Marcus, Lisa Parks, Ellen Seiter, Cameron McCarthy, Paula Treichler, David Kennedy, Rob Nixon, Arvind Rajagopal, Cristina Venegas, George Yúdice, Tom Streeter, Larry Gross, Kelly Gates, Herman Gray, Rick Maxwell, Faye Ginsburg, Michael Hanchard, James Hay, and Mike Curtin. They operated across anthropology, law, sociology, education, political science, and literary, area, and communication studies.[5]

If you accept this account, it might seem as though things are very much in accord with Hoggart's heritage and the yet more radical inspiration of Antonio Gramsci, with culture a terrain of struggle for hegemony. In the words of the venerable German Socialist rallying cry, a "Long March of the Institutions" was under way (Mansfield 1990). But cultural-policy studies and cultural studies begat creative-industries discourse. How, where, and why did that happen, and with what effect?

The turn to creative industries is a reaction to the prevailing political economy described earlier. As per Reagan's doctrine, right across the United States, municipal, regional, and state funding agencies have dropped old funding and administrative categories of arts and crafts, replacing them with the discourse of the creative industries. The same thing has happened in Europe, Latin America, Africa, and Asia. In 2006, Rwanda convened a global conference on the "Creative Economy" to commodify/govern the social healing engendered by culture. Brazil houses the United Nations Conference on Trade and Development (UNCTAD) and the United Nations Development Program's International Forum for Creative Industries. Even India's venerable last gasp of Nehruvianism, its Planning Commission, has a committee for creative industries (Ramanathan 2006; United Nations Conference on Trade and Development 2004: 7). China has moved "from an older, state-dominated focus on cultural industries . . . towards a more market-oriented pattern of creative industries" (Keane 2006), and Singapore, Hong Kong, Japan, and South Korea have similar strategies (Peichi 2008; Cunningham 2009c). True believers argue for an efflorescence of creativity, cultural difference, import substitu-

---

5. Again, I was involved with several of these formations.

tion, and national and regional pride and influence, thanks to new technologies and innovative firms (Cunningham 2001, 2009a).

The change is also an intellectual one. The creative-industries humanities correspond to a great appeal, a grand passion of the age. They herald a new interdisciplinarity that blends research production, technical innovation, and social inclusiveness, embedding universities in everyday life (Brint et al. 2009 describe this tendency). Humanities professors already interested in policy for reasons of cultural nationalism, or in opposition to corporate rule, take the opportunity to sit near the heart of power, transcending their traditional status as "the little match seller, nose pressed to the window, looking in on the grand life within" (Cunningham 2006a). Many have shifted their discourse to a copyright-inflected one, focusing on comparative advantage and competition rather than heritage and aesthetics. Neoliberal emphases on creativity have succeeded old-school cultural patrimony. The capacity of the market to govern everything contrasts with cultural policy's limited purview, opening up a new life world to obedient rhetoricians.

Cunningham no longer speaks of mixing socialist ideals with reformism. He favors "a better matching of curriculum to career" via "practical business challenges" such that "non-market disciplines" (I assume that means much of the humanities, cell biology, zoology, particle acceleration—you name it) generate internal markets in competition with others and forge "an alliance with the business sector" (2009b, 2007b, 2007a). This is a true believer having a second Damascene moment. The *converso* from psychoanalysis and cultural nationalism in the 1980s to cultural policy in the 1990s realized, Gloucester-like, that he stumbled when he saw. Fortunately, he was blinded again. *This* time, with his sight returned in a twenty-first-century epiphany, he *really* knows what's going on.[6] The Australian Research Council, which once supported a major cultural-policy initiative under the Gramscian-turned-Foucauldian Bennett, now funds

---

6. Noel King (pers. comm., 2011) reminds me that Stuart never lost his faith in Girardian mimetic desire. And I should add that I have immeasurable admiration for Stuart's own research and his ethics, if not for their ideological and political-economic articulation.

a pioneering Centre of Excellence for Creative Industries and Innovation (CCI), founded by Cunningham and the lapsed semiotic romantic and Bennite John Hartley (see http://www.cci.edu.au). The CCI even invents new forms of language, as when it solemnly announces "an industry facing spin-off from the centre's mapping work, Creative Business Benchmarker" (Cunningham 2011).

These powerful advocates are in thrall to the idea that culture is an endlessly growing resource capable of dynamizing society. UNCTAD decrees that "creativity, more than labor and capital, or even traditional technologies, is deeply embedded in every country's cultural context" (2004: 3). UNESCO's Global Alliance for Cultural Diversity (2002) heralds creative industries as a portmanteau term that covers the cultural sector and goes further, beyond output and into that favorite neoliberal canard of process. In the same vein, the Australian Academy for the Humanities calls for "research in the humanities and creative arts" to be tax-exempt, based on its contribution to research and development, and subject to the same surveys of "employer demand" as the professions and the sciences (2010; also see Cunningham 2007a). Even the prosaic National Research Council (NRC) of the U.S. National Academies notes that the electronic media play "a crucial role in culture," offering "personal, social, and educational benefit" and "economic development" (Mitchell, Inouye, and Blumenthal 2003: 1). Snow's cultural divide is truly imperiled when we are told, with staggering brio, that concerns about labor are passé as evolutionary economics gushes over the number of billionaires in their thirties involved in the creative industries. This is said to presage the evolution of a new, entrepreneurial sector in "an open economy and an open society" (Potts 2006: 339). Some might regard their emergence as a sign of class politics structured in dominance. How quaintly old-fashioned that would be.

For its part, the British Academy seeks to understand and further the "creative and cultural industries" (2004: viii). In partnership with the AHRC, the U.K.'s National Endowment for Science, Technology and the Arts (NESTA) says that "the arts and humanities have a particularly strong affiliation with the creative industries" and provide research that "helps to fuel" them, in turn boosting innovation more broadly (Bakhshi, Schneider, and Walker 2008: 1). The AHRC (2010) places a high priority on intensely applied, materially measurable forms of knowledge. Its mission is worth quoting at some length:

> In the current climate of tighter spending reviews and constraints on public spending there is an increased focus on demonstrating the economic, social and cultural benefits of publicly-funded research to wider society. . . .
>
> The arts and humanities create social and economic benefits directly and indirectly through improvements in social and intellectual capital, social networking, community identity, learning and skills and quality of life. The diverse set of impacts includes enhancing the knowledge economy, providing innovative content and support for the creative and cultural industries, enhancing public debates, participation and engagement, informing developments in performance, professional practice or public policy and contributing to regeneration, community cohesion and social inclusion. . . .
>
> In thinking about potential impacts, it may be helpful to consider the potential beneficiaries of the research:
>
> - Are there potential beneficiaries within the private sector?
> - Is there anyone, including policy-makers, within international, national, local or devolved government and government agencies who would benefit from the research?
> - Are there potential beneficiaries within the public sector, third sector or any others (e.g. museums, galleries, charities)?
> - Would the research be of interest to professional or practitioner groups (such as the legal profession, architects, planners, archivists, designers, creative and performing artists)[?]
> - Are there any beneficiaries within the wider public?

I'm a fan particularly of the "Is there anyone" out there clause. Very Pink Floyd.

The U.S. President's Committee on Arts and the Humanities (2010) heralds the "Creative Economy" as a central focus of its activities, stressing that "the President's Committee focuses its leadership, with other agencies and the private sector, on the power of the arts and humanities as an economic driver, sustaining critical cultural resources and fostering civic investment in cultural assets and infrastructure. These efforts help speed innovation and expand markets and consumers, directly benefiting local economies." As we have seen, this rhetoric has not stimulated the humanities budget. Even though Reagan birthed the discourse of creative industries, the U.S. academy is behind the times due to the disabling division of the two humanities and their disarticulation from public policy. Our local and state governments may be shifting cultural categories, but we are oblivious to the fact. The NEH (2010) flails about via "Humanities Initiatives at Institutions with High Hispanic Enrollment" that privilege "connections to professional training (in such fields as medicine, nursing, technology, business, law, and economics)," but it forbids scholars to participate in "creative or performing arts; empirical social science research; specific policy studies" or "projects devoted to advocacy." Such prohibitions are absurd, a last gasp of Humanities One binarism. Are we seriously supposed to think that technology, business, economics, and the law operate outside performance, policy, and advocacy, or that Latin@s must abjure the substance of identity formation even as their identity formation is supposedly being privileged?

In the British and Australian cases, considerable controversy has arisen from creative-industries discourse. As the conventional humanities grew distant from working- and lower-middle-class college life, and the U.K. government withdrew teaching grants from the sector, the conventional humanities grew dependent on tuition to sustain research at a time when fees began to vary across fields in ways that did not relate to the cost of mounting classes. Disciplines in demand at a policy level were expected to subsidize the humanities, which were more popular with students. And the AHRC prioritized research that studied the ruling Conservative Party's "big society," an alias for rolling back the state. The arms-length Haldane principle of funding was thus "clarified" to ensure obedience to policy priorities and party slogans. The quid pro quo saw the government shield the council from budget cuts (Independent Review of Higher Education Funding and Student Finance 2010; Morgan 2011; Skerritt 2011; Swain 2011; Boffey 2011; Brooks 2011).

The Creative Response

In a First Wave economy, land and farm labor are the main "factors of production." In a Second Wave economy, the land remains valuable while the "labor" becomes massified around machines and larger industries. In a Third Wave economy, the central resource—a single word broadly encompassing data, information, images, symbols, culture, ideology, and values—is actionable knowledge.
    —Esther Dyson, George Gilder, George Keyworth, and Alvin Toffler,
    "A Magna Carta for the Information Age"

What does all this mean on the ground? In the words of lapsed-leftist cultural theorist and inaugural president of the European Bank for Reconstruction and Development Jacques Attali, a new "mercantile order forms wherever a creative class masters a key innovation from navigation to accounting or, in our own time, where services are most efficiently mass produced, thus generating enormous wealth" (2008: 31). This allegedly gives rise to an "aristocracy of talent" (Kotkin 2001: 22) in which multiple meritocrats luxuriate in ever-changing techniques, technologies, and networks. Labor is acknowledged in this brave newness, provided that it is abstracted from physical, dirty work (Mattelart 2002).

The high priest of creative-industries discourse, business professor Richard Florida (2002), speaks of a "creative class®" that is revitalizing postindustrial towns in the Global North devastated by the relocation of agriculture and manufacturing to places with cheaper labor pools. The revival of such cities, Florida argues, is driven by a magic elixir of tolerance, technology, and talent, as measured by same-sex households, broadband connections, and higher degrees in successful postindustrial regions. As a performative point, he has even trademarked the very concept: The registration number for "creative class®" with the U.S. Patent and Trademark Office (2012) is 3298801 (see http://tess2.uspto.gov/bin/showfield?f=doc&state=4005: 8s6e9.3.1).[7]

A neoliberal bequest of creativity has succeeded the old-school patrimony of culture, because economic transformations have comprehensively challenged the idea of the humanities as removed from in-

---

7. Thanks to Bill Grantham for directing me to the office's Trademark Electronic Search System (TESS).

dustry. The comparatively cheap and easy access to making and distributing meaning afforded by Internet media and genres is thought to have eroded the one-way hold on culture that saw a small segment of the world as producers and the larger segment as consumers. The result is said to be a democratized media, higher skill levels, more sovereign customers, and powerful challenges to old patterns of expertise and institutional authority. Creativity is distributed rather than centralized. It becomes both a pleasure and a responsibility to invest in one's own human capital—signs of a robust civil society and private self.

The working assumption is that the culture industries are being overrun by individual creativity. It's a Marxist/Godardian fantasy. People fish, film, fuck, and finance from morning to midnight. Media technologies obliterate geography, sovereignty, and hierarchy in an alchemy of truth and beauty. A deregulated, individuated world makes consumers into producers, frees people who are disabled from confinement, encourages new subjectivities, rewards intellect and competitiveness, links people across cultures, and allows billions of flowers to bloom in a postpolitical cornucopia. Consumption is privileged, production is discounted, and labor is forgotten (Dahlström and Hermelin 2007; Ritzer and Jurgenson 2010).

Creative-industry academics have become branded celebrities. Descending on welcoming burghers eager to be made over at public expense by professors whose books appear on airport newsstands rather than cloistered scholarly shelves, these carpetbagging, white-shoe consultants sidestep the historic tasks laid out by the left (Gibson and Klocker 2004). For a date with Florida, see http://www.creative class.com; should you wish to hear Attali at your next convention, he can be contacted at the Global Speakers Bureau (http://www.speak ers.co.uk/our-speakers/profile/Jacques_Attali). Save your pennies to pay for the privilege.

Prone to cybertarianism, chorines of digital capitalism and the technological sublime pile out of business class and onto the Jetway in three major groups. Richard Floridians hop a limousine from the airport and then ride around town on bicycles to spy on ballet-loving, gay-friendly, multicultural computer geeks who have relocated to deindustrialized, freezing rust belts. True-believer Australian creationists criticize cultural-policy studies as residually socialistic and textual. And Brussels bureaucrats offer blueprints to cities eager for affluence and prepared to be reinvented via culture and tolerance. All promise a makeover "from the rusty coinage of 'cultural industries' to newly minted 'creative industries'" (Ross 2006–2007: 1). Their scholarly work rarely cites books, often cites web pages, and always endorses "reports."

In part, the changes they have wrought and represent signify the interdisciplinarity that Snow favored—and I think the humanities need. But he also fought for ordinary people "lost in the great anonymous sludge of history," where life, he said (troping Hobbes) "has always been nasty, brutish and short" (1987: 26–27, 42). In his commentary on Snow, Pynchon (1984) defended old-style Luddites. Far from protesting new technology, they opposed well-established machinery that had shed jobs over two centuries. Ned Lud was no "technophobic crazy." He simply recognized that men who did not do productive work controlled the lives of those who *did* work. These concerns still matter. They have gone sorely missing in later developments.

Today's discourse on the creative industries ignores such critical issues as the cognitariat, high-tech pollution, and cultural imperialism, not to mention the need to *understand* industries rather than celebrate them. For instance, the service and cultural industries of the "new" economy supposedly represent clean business. The Australian Council for the Humanities, Arts and Social Sciences' submission to its national Productivity Commission refers to a "post-smokestack era" (CHASS 2006)—a utopia for workers, consumers, and residents with residues of code, not carbon. Yet the Political Economy Research Institute's 2004 *Misfortune 100: Top Corporate Air Polluters in the United States* placed media owners at numbers 1, 3, 16, 22, and 39. Media production relies on the exorbitant water use of computer technology, while making semiconductors requires hazardous chemicals, including carcinogens. Waste from discarded electronics is one of the biggest sources of heavy metals and toxic pollutants in the world's trash piles. The accumulation of electronic hardware causes grave environmental and health concerns, stemming from the potential seepage of noxious chemicals, gases, and metals into landfills and water sources. Much e-waste recycling is exported. California alone shipped about twenty million pounds of electronic waste in 2006 to Malaysia, Brazil, South Korea, China, Mexico, Viet Nam, and India, where preteen girls pick away without protection at discarded televisions and computers, looking for precious metals to sell, with the remains dumped in landfills (Maxwell and Miller 2012). The creative industries generate a lot of detritus.

There are also definitional and hence statistical problems with the very concept. The assumption that what is made in a sector of the economy does not *characterize* that sector, that "creativity" is not an input but an industry's defining quality, is misleading. A bizarre shift in adjectival meaning makes it possible for anything profitable to be catalogued under "creative." More precise efforts at definition have significantly diminished the claims made for the sector's economic contributions, unmasking the boosterist sleight of hand that places the humanities at the center of economic innovation by pretending that they encompass corporate and governmental information technology (Miller 2009b; Garnham 2005). Aware of this searing lack, true believers have generated a figure of speech designed to counter it via the "creative trident" (an aptly militaristic metaphor given the humanities' heritage): "The 'creative trident' methodology . . . is the total of creative occupations within the core creative industries (specialists), plus the creative occupations employed in other industries (embedded) plus the business and support occupations employed in creative industries who are often responsible for managing, for and technically supporting creative activity (support)" (Cunningham 2011: 25).

It's obvious that big firms rarely innovate. That's hardly news. But it is inaccurate to regard that fact as a shift in the center of gravity. The cultural industries remain under the control of media and communications conglomerates, who gobble up smaller firms that invent products and services. We must also ask whether creative-industries discourse amounts to "recycling audio-visual cultural material created by the grassroots genius, exploiting their intellectual property and generating a standardized business sector that excludes, and even distorts, its very source of business" (Ramanathan 2006). The beneficiaries of innovations by "talented amateurs" are, once again, corporations (Ross 2006–2007; C. Marcus 2005).

The supposedly brave new world raises several questions for me: Is it revolutionary, scholarly, innovative, or creative to buy on Amazon, be known through Facebook, sell via Craig's List, travel with Apple appliances, look for truth on Google, or get news from the BBC (things that people spend a lot of time doing on the Internet)? Who owns http://www.last.fm, http://www.rottentomatoes.com, and http://www.youtube.com? (Viacom, Time Warner, and Google.)

And there is minimal proof that a creative class exists and "creative cities" outperform their drab brethren economically. Companies seek skills when deciding where to locate their businesses—but skills also seek work. City centers largely attract the young who are not yet breeding. The centrality of gay culture in the Floridian calculus derives from assuming same-sex households are queer (but university dorms and sorority/fraternity houses are not quite there). Even if this were accurate, many 'successful' U.S. cities roll with reaction (consider Orlando and Phoenix). The idea of urbanism incipient in U.S. demographic statistics includes the suburbs (which now hold more residents than do cities), so that, too, is suspect in terms of the importance of downtown lofts to economies. There is no evidence of an overlap of tastes, values, living arrangements, or locations between artists and accountants, despite their being bundled together in the creative concept; nor is it sensible to assume other countries replicate the massive internal mobility of the U.S. population. Finally, other surveys pour scorn on the claim that quality of life, rather than low cost, good communications technology, proximity to markets, and adequate transport, is central to selecting business campuses. A European Commission evaluation of twenty-nine Cities of Culture disclosed that their principal goal—economic growth stimulated by the public subvention of culture to renew failed cities—has itself failed. Glasgow, for instance, was initially hailed as a success of the program; but many years after the rhetoric, it has seen no sustained growth. When Liverpool became an official City of Culture in 2008, it allocated £3 billion in public funds to an arts program, a museum, galleries, a convention center, a retail outlet, renewed transportation, rebuilt waterfront, and every good thing, premised on regeneration through culture. Skeptics were right to ask, "Is that a foundation strong enough to sustain a lasting economy? Or . . . pyramid selling?" (Nathan 2005; Hoggart 2005:

168; Linklater 2006; K. Oakley 2006, 2004; David Bell 2007; Freeman 2007; Huijgh 2007; Peck 2007; Ross 2006–2007).

At best, creative-industries discourse is offering itself as "an industry training program" (Turner 2012). At worst, it is helping perpetuate massively stratified labor markets for the production of culture (K. Oakley, forthcoming). It has proven to be an exciting, innovative, but problematic way of taking up Snow's provocation; a stimulating model for overcoming the divide of the two humanities that requires caution rather than cathexis.

In the United States, the prevailing ideology of creative industries may not have overwhelmed the humanities in general, but it is orthodox in one particular sector. This next section examines the unfortunate way in which creative-industries discourse exemplifies the collapse of the Two Cultures' binary form, upgrading the humanities' long-standing contribution to martial masculinity and legitimizing the precarious employment of the cognitariat.

Recruiting for the Great Game and the Cognitariat

Blackwell is what his creators call an interactive virtual character—
a life-sized, 3-D simulation of a person whose mission is to help train
real soldiers. He inhabits FlatWorld, a kind of theme-park version
of a war zone run by the University of Southern California's [USC]
Institute for Creative Technologies [ICT].

At a time when Hollywood is often tagged by those on the
political right as a liberal bastion, ICT teams the military and the
entertainment biz for defense projects, funded by a five-year, $100
million grant from the Pentagon—the largest the university has ever
received.

—James Hebert, "Band of Brothers"

We have seen that the upshot of creative-industries discourse is market objectives overdetermining cultural ones. This tendency is exemplified in electronic or video games, which have broken down barriers between the sciences and humanities and confirmed the latter's role in molding martial masculinity and the cognitariat, as universities seek some of the Pentagon's $6 billion annual expenditure on the virtual and apply their mimetic managerial model across industries (Singer

2010). The U.K.'s AHRC and NESTA identify games as a prime "example of where the creative industries make a significant contribution to the economy" and why they should be central to research priorities (Bakhshi, Schneider, and Walker 2008: 9). Even the National Endowment for the Arts (NEA; n.d.) underwrites them. And so does imperialism.

Powerful ties between universities, the media, and militarism go back a long way. The Armed Forces Communications and Electronics Association began in 1946 (http://www.afcea.org). In 1967, J. William Fulbright (1972) updated Eisenhower's (1972) warning of a "military-industrial complex" in declaring the existence of a fully-fledged "military-industrial-academic complex."

Matters have heated up since then and not just in the usual domains. In 1996, the National Academy of Sciences held a workshop for academia, Hollywood, and the Pentagon on simulation and games. The next year, the NRC announced a collaborative research agenda on popular culture and militarism and convened meetings to streamline such cooperation, from special effects to training simulations, from immersive technologies to simulated networks. And since 2001, gaming has become a crucial tool tactically and strategically as fewer and fewer nations permit the United States to play live war games (Lenoir 2003: 190; Macedonia 2002; Kundnani 2004).

As part of these developments, untold numbers of academic journals and institutes have tethered themselves to the Pentagon, generating research designed to test and augment the recruitment and training potential of games to ideologize, hire, and instruct the population. The Center for Computational Analysis of Social and Organizational Systems at Carnegie Mellon University in Pittsburgh (http://www.casos.cs.cmu.edu), for example, promulgates studies underwritten by the Office of Naval Research and the Defense Advanced Research Projects Agency (DARPA). DARPA's wonderful slogan is "Creating and Preventing Strategic Surprise" (see http://www.darpa.mil). And the Association for the Advancement of Artificial Intelligence (a "scientific society") parades similar work (see http://www.aaai.org/AITopics/Military).

USC's ICT was set up in 1998 in my beloved, benighted, lonesome home of Los Angeles to articulate faculty, film and television producers, game designers, and the defense budget. Film school meets fighter jet, if you like. Formally opened by the secretary of the army and the head of the Motion Picture Association of America, the institute had a workspace dreamed up by the set designer for the *Star Trek* franchise and $45 million in military money, a figure that was doubled in its 2004 renewal and extended in 2011 to $135 million over three years. In other words, ICT uses Pentagon loot and Hollywood muscle to test out homicidal technologies and narrative scenarios under the aegis of film, engineering, theater, and communications professors. By the end of 2010, its products were available on sixty-five military bases (Deck 2004; Silver and Marwick 2006: 50; Turse 2008: 120; Hennigan 2010; Institute for Creative Technologies 2011).[8]

The institute also collaborates on major motion pictures, for instance, *Spider-Man 2* (Sam Raimi, 2004), and produces military recruitment tools such as *Full Spectrum Warrior* that double as "training devices for military operations in urban terrain": What's good for the Xbox is good for the combat simulator. The utility of these innovations continues in the field. The Pentagon is aware that off-duty soldiers play games. It wants to invade their supposed leisure time and wean them from the skater genre in favor of what are essentially training manuals. The Department of Defense (DOD) even boasts that *Full Spectrum Warrior* was the "game that captured Saddam," because the men who dug Saddam Hussein Abd al-Majid al-Tikriti out had played it (Burston 2003; Stockwell and Muir 2003; Andersen 2007; Turse 2008: 122, 119; Harmon 2003; Dyer-Witheford and de Peuter 2009).

To keep up with the institute's work, you can listen to podcasts from *Armed with Science: Research and Applications for the Modern Military* via the DOD (http://science.dodlive.mil). You will learn that the Pentagon and USC are developing *UrbanSim* to improve "the art of battle command" as part of Obama's imperial wars. It is described as a small shift from commercial gaming: "Instead of having Godzilla and tornados attacking your city, the players are faced with things like uncooperative local officials and ethnic divisions in the communities, different tribal rivalries," to quote an institute scholar in the pod

---

8. We should note that there is skepticism about the actual efficacy of such work as military training (Newsome and Lewis 2011).

(Department of Defense 2010). You might also visit ICT's Twitter address (@usc_ict), website (http://ict.usc.edu), and Facebook page (http://www.facebook.com/USCICT), where hortatory remarks of self-regard abound to an extent rarely seen in the postwar era: The institute "is revolutionizing learning through the development of interactive digital media" because by "collaborating with our entertainment industry neighbors, we are leaders in producing virtual humans," thereby furthering "cultural awareness, leadership and health." That means servicing the Pentagon. For despite the fact that ICT (which has stopped replying to my requests for a visit) says its "innovations help save lives," it is dedicated to life-destroying war machinery, not life-saving public health.

Digging a little further, one can test out these putatively life-saving technologies courtesy of LabTV "Sergeant Star," a virtual recruiter developed by the institute's marvelously named Mixed Reality Research and Development wing as a means of attracting gormless youth to serve. Sergeant Star is disingenuously described as "a new class of virtual human guide" animated by "Hollywood storytelling techniques" whose "personality matches his good looks" (hint: white, square-jawed) (Institute for Creative Technologies 2012).

For its part, the Naval Postgraduate School's Modeling, Virtual Environments, and Simulation Academic Program (http://www.movesinstitute.org) developed a game called *Operation Starfighter*, based on the film *The Last Starfighter* (Nick Castle, 1984). The next step was farmed out to George Lucas's companies, inter alia. *America's Army* was launched with due symbolism on July 4, 2002—dually symbolic in that Independence Day doubles as a key date in the film industry's summer rollout of features. The military had to bring additional servers into play to handle four hundred thousand downloads of the game that first day. *Gamespot PC Reviews* awarded it a high textual rating and was equally impressed by the "business model." Needless to say, the *America's Army* community (http://americasarmy.com/community) takes full advantage of the usual array of cybertarian fantasies about the new media as civil society, across the gamut of community fora, Internet chats, fan sites, and virtual competitions. And the game is formally commodified through privatization—bought by Ubisoft to be repurposed for consoles, arcades, and cell phones and turned into figurines by the allegedly edgy independent company Radioactive Clown. Tournaments are convened, replete with hundreds of thousands of dollars in prize money, along with smaller events at military recruiting sites ("AA:SF" 2008; Power 2007: 279–80; Turse 2008: 117, 123–24; Lenoir 2003: 175).

A decade after its release, *America's Army* remains one of the ten most-played games online, with millions of registered users. Civilian developers regularly refresh it by consulting with veterans and participating in physical war games. Paratexts provide additional promotional renewal. With over forty million downloads, and websites by the thousands, its message has traveled far and wide—an excellent return on the initial public investment of $19 million and $3.5 million for annual updates. Studies of young people who have positive attitudes to the U.S. military indicate that 30 percent of them formed that view through playing the game—a game that sports a Teen rating, forbids role reversal via modifications (preventing players from experiencing the pain of the other), and is officially ranked first among the army's recruiting tools (Nieborg 2004; Turse 2008: 118, 157; Craig 2006; Shachtman 2002; Thompson 2004; Goodman 2009). The Pentagon is very keen to undertake surveillance of teenage players' practices and interests to uncover "top America's Army players' distinct behaviours, the optimum size of an America's Army team, the importance of fire volume toward opponent, the recommendable communication structure and content, and the contribution of the unity among team members" (Carley et al. 2005).

For all its love of the ICT, DARPA likes to spread the fiscal joy of its $2 billion annual budget around universities (Defense Advanced Research Projects Agency, "Universities," n.d.). It refers to Orlando as "Team Orlando" because the city houses Disney's research-and-development "imagineers," the University of Central Florida's Institute for Simulation and Training, and Lockheed Martin (the nation's biggest military contractor, whose trademark is "We never forget who we're working for"; see http://teamorlando.org/about/index.shtml and http://www.lockheedmartin.com). Away from the spectacular world of combat, faculty spend time spicing up the drab lives of Pentagon office workers by designing games such as *Treasure Cheese* and *Procurement Fraud Indicators* (Ackerman 2010) in concert with the

absurdly named Defense Acquisitions University (http://www.dau
.mil/default.aspx).

In short, gaming and universities are connected through "technological nationalism" (Charland 1986). Complicit campuses have
formed a symbiotic ideological and material relationship with what
is also, by the way, probably the globe's leading polluter—the DOD.
Military deployment of electronics, information technologies, games,
and special effects links higher education to the Pentagon's orgiastic
use of fossil fuels, destruction of terrain and infrastructure, radiation,
conventional pollution, buried ordnance, defoliants, land use, anti-
personnel mines, carcinogenic chemical deposits, and toxic effluents.
Despite latter-day claims that it is "going green," the DOD remains
the world's largest user of petroleum (Shachtman 2010; Corbett and
Turco 2006; Leaning 2000; Jorgenson, Clark, and Kentor 2010).

Meanwhile, virtual blowback is under way, with al-Qaeda re-
portedly learning tactics by playing these games and developing
counters of its own (Power 2007: 283), Islam Games thriving (http://
islamgames.com), Hezbollah offering *Special Force 2* (Singer 2010),
and Joseph DeLappe (2006) creating countertexts online by typing
personal details of deceased soldiers into *America's Army* under the
moniker "dead-in-iraq."

University scholars involved with Pentagon paymasters would
do well to read some scientific history. In his testimony to the U.S.
Atomic Energy Commission, the noted physicist J. Robert Oppenheimer, who led the group that developed the atomic bomb, talked
about the instrumental rationality that animated the people who created this awesome technology. Once his team of scientists saw that it
was feasible, the device's impact lost intellectual and emotional significance for them. They had been overtaken by its "technically sweet"
quality (United States Atomic Energy Commission 1954: 81).

Just such techno-saccharine is the lifeblood of the creative industries' instrumental pleasure and exhilarating utopia. "Technically
sweet" qualities animate innovation, adoption, and the mix of the
sublime—the awesome, the ineffable, the uncontrollable, and the powerful—with the beautiful—the approachable, the attractive, the pli-
ant, and the soothing. In philosophical aesthetics, the sublime and the
beautiful are generally regarded as opposites. But game technologies

have helped bring them together for ICT denizens and their creative-industry friends across campuses in an alchemy of murderous phenomenological play and aesthetic production values.

Recognizing that fact should lead us to a next step. The American Academy of Pediatrics (2009) denounces the mimetic impact of violent electronic games on young people yet disgracefully fails to note that this is preyed on by the DOD. As per the brave actions taken by professional bodies in anthropology and—belatedly—psychology against their co-optation by the U.S. war machine (see American Anthropological Association 2006), we must shame universities for their role in electronic-gaming militarism (see LeVine 2011 for the social sciences' complicity with slaughter; their earlier history is explained in Simpson 1998). USC and Carnegie Mellon academics should protest the bloody work of empire undertaken on their campuses, collectively and publicly. We must all contest DARPA's ideological incorporation of untenured faculty, whom it seeks to engage via a "Young Faculty Award" that aims "to develop the next generation of academic scientists, engineers and mathematicians in key disciplines who will focus a significant portion of their career on DoD and national security issues" (Defense Advanced Research Projects Agency, "Opportunities," n.d.). Faculty in other countries need to consider boycotts of military-endowed U.S. universities and researchers if we fail to refuse these murderous paymasters. The latest humanities contribution to martial masculinity is very, very dangerous.

The Cognitariat

In addition to the military impact of these deadly devices, universities are complicit in an industry that is destabilizing labor rights. The college-trained cognitariat plays key roles in the production and circulation of goods and services, creating and coordinating media technologies and texts. The prevailing ideology of capitalist futurism that underpins this cognitariat requires correction. As Herbert Marcuse (1941) predicted seventy years ago, far from liberating all and sundry, technological convergence has intensified managerial coordination from above. Writing in this critical neo-Marxist tradition contra Cold-Warrior futurists, Herbert I. Schiller recast cultural and technological convergence as an "infrastructure of socialization." Designed to spread from rich countries to poor ones, it synchronized "business cultures," organizational models, "institutional networks," and communication and cultural production (1976: 8–9, 16).

How does this play out when eager humanities undergrads enter the games industry? They encounter big publishers who have developed exploitative work practices as their power has increased via the destruction or purchase of small businesses. The labor process inside these places starts when someone builds a demonstration model and shows it to a company, which previews it to the press. In any given year, a firm generally decides to ready a game in time for Christmas sales. By March, it requires workers to be present sixty hours a week, with the promise of a bonus when the game is shipped. Then management goes over the game and insists on changes. In June, people are working eighty hours a week. Then the company finds the product will not be available by Christmas. It shifts shipment to the following March but keeps everyone working at the same rate. The bonus migrates months into the future. A putatively limited "pre-crunch" is announced in the period before release of a new game. Forty-eight-hour weeks are required, with the alibi that months of this obviate the need for a real "crunch" at the conclusion of development. The pre-crunch lasts beyond its deadline, and seventy-two-hour weeks are mandated. That crunch passes its promised end, illness and irritability strike, and a new crunch is announced: Everyone must work eighty-five- to ninety-one-hour weeks, 9:00 A.M. to 10:00 P.M. Monday to Sunday inclusive, with the (occasional) Saturday evening off, after 6:30 P.M. There is no overtime or leave in return for this massive expenditure of talent and time (Dyer-Witheford and de Peuter, 2006; Schumacher 2006–2007; anonymous informant, 2005; Waters 2007).

Consider the notorious case of Electronic Arts (EA). EA is based in California, with "worldwide studios" in British Columbia and offshoots in Canada, Hong Kong, Tokyo, China, and Britain, inter alia. EA makes *The Sims*, National Hockey League games, *FIFA World Cup*, and the John Madden "football" franchise. Trip Hawkins founded the company in 1982. He dismissed broadcast television as "brain-deadening" and embraced "interactive media" as a development "that would connect people and help them grow." Not surprisingly, and in best cybertarian fashion, EA emphasizes art and technology under the sign of publishing. Its developers were initially promoted as authors: *M.U.L.E.* and *Murder on the Zinderneuf* were marketed through their designers' names, as were rock albums of the day. Shining white designing youths were celebrated in a famous 1983 advertisement called "We See Farther." But geek authorship was soon supplanted. By the mid-1980s, the "authors" of key games were no longer dweebs in black polo necks but Doctor J (Julius Erving) and Larry Bird (basketball celebrities brought in as endorsers/faux designers). Creators lost their moment of fame. Since that time, a stream of sports stories has drawn on promotions underwritten by others' creativity and money, displacing what came to be regarded as the esoteric pursuits of the first innovators (Cifaldi and Fleming 2007).

EA proceeded to buy development studios and set up design teams on an industrial model. At the same time, it sought to undermine the existing political economy of the industry by cutting discounts to distributors of software, thereby building up revenues. The next move was to write games for personal computers and consoles and become a distributor. In addition to continuing with console options, in the late 1990s EA entered virtual worlds and awakened to female consumers, buying advertising space and time across fashion periodicals and TV aimed at young women. The company became massively successful—2007 revenues were $3.091 billion. It boasted almost eight thousand employees and began buying other studios. After it lost preeminence to Activision-Blizzard in 2009–2010, the stock price fell, but a switch from depending on console games readied this oleaginous firm to stimulate and satisfy the desire of young men for virtual killing via mobile devices. EA even got over Hawkins's snobbish dismissal of TV, since gamers love television and want to integrate it with their thumbs (Cifaldi and Fleming 2007; Cadin, Guérin, and DeFillippi 2006; C. Morris 2011).

In 2004, however, the company became a byword for the poor labor practices that characterize the sector. A blogger going under the sobriquet of "ea_spouse" posted a vibrant account of the exploitation experienced by her fiancé and others working for the firm (ea_spouse 2004). Eloquently ripping back the veneer of joyous cybertarianism from games development, she disclosed that EA's claim to blend aesthetics and technology, according to its name and corporate trademark—"Challenge Everything"—belied both its treatment of employees and its products. Of labor, she wrote, "To any EA executive that happens to read this, I have a good challenge for you: how about safe and sane labor practices for the people on whose backs you walk for your millions?" Of texts: "Churning out one licensed football game after another doesn't sound like challenging much of anything to me; it sounds like a money farm" (also see Dyer-Witheford and de Peuter 2006; Schumacher 2006–2007).

At the very moment that ea_spouse blew the whistle, *Fortune* magazine was ranking her fiancé's employer among the "100 Best Companies to Work For" (Levering et al. 2003). EA came sixty-second in the magazine's "List of Industry Stars" (2007) and ninety-first among firms that "try hard to do right by their staff," as measured by the Great Place to Work Institute. EA called itself "a one-class society." Its vice president of human resources at the time, Rusty Rueff, operated with the following dictum: "Most creativity comes at one of two times: When your back is up against the wall or in a time of calm." In case readers found repeated firing-squad analogies alarming, *Fortune* reassured them that workers could "refresh their energy with free espresso or by playing volleyball and basketball." Today, EA games president Frank Gibeau informs potential investors that "we're on the offensive. We're moving from a fire-and-forget packaged goods model to an online services model." Despite these wonders, the exploitation begat class-action lawsuits that saw the funsters pay $30 million for overdue overtime based on the fact that employees "do not perform work that is original or creative" because they are "seldom allowed to use their own judgment" (Dyer-Witheford and de Peuter 2006; C. Morris 2011; Surette 2006; for additional scandal, see Bohannon 2008). EA's website continues to blather on about its labor record but not in terms of the class action—rather, that it fares well on the Human Rights Campaign's Corporate Equality Index. I think that means it is as committed to deskilling queer people as straight people. Very Floridian.

The intervention (as we say in cultural studies) or outburst (as they say elsewhere) of ea_spouse generated febrile and substantial responses, such as calls for unionization, appeals to federal and state labor machinery, confirmation that EA was horrendous but by no means aberrant, frustration that the bourgeois press was disinclined to investigate or even report the situation, denunciations of asinine managerialism and private-sector bureaucracy (for example, "the average game company manager is quite possibly the worst qualified leader of people in the world"), and a recognition that intellectual property rights make labor disposable ("I'm beginning to think that EA is really nothing more than a licensing warehouse. They'll always be able to recruit naïve talent to slave away. . . . Alienating talent is not a big problem for them"). For a time, ea_spouse ran a website replete with horror stories by angry former idealists from all over the globe who thought they were doing "cool stuff" until they experienced webshop horror.

Labor solidarity for these creative workers remains compromised by job threats from around the world and nondisclosure agreements from around the company, which send a chill through conversations across employment silos (Waters 2007). As more and more families complain about the impact of making sweated games, the right responds with the splendid "Real Housewives of Game Development" (2011) created by the conglomerate IGN (2011), which describes itself as "obsessed with gaming, entertainment and everything guys enjoy." Party on, humanities dudes. The next chapter focuses on how one might navigate this new terrain more "creatively," shall we say.

A Third Humanities

The idea that the media aren't worth studying is as foolish as the idea, which survived into the 20th century at elite universities and public schools, that science and engineering were not proper subjects for young gentlemen. The media industries, apart from their contribution to G[ross]D[omestic]P[roduct], now impinge on people's lives to an extent unimaginable even 20 years ago. . . . Some education in the media is surely essential. But it suits the industry's owners if citizens lack the skills and knowledge to sustain critical attitudes.
—Peter Wilby, "I Sued and Won"

There are full professors in this place who read nothing but cereal boxes. . . . It's the only avant garde we've got.
—Don DeLillo, *White Noise*

The wealthier white population is aging and diminishing in size and the younger, poorer, expanding population tends to be black and increasingly Latino. . . . Vocal resistance to public funding for education has grown notably sharper.
—David Theo Goldberg, "The AfterLife of the Humanities"

As we think about the frantic defensive measures adopted by true believers in Humanities One and the earnest co-optive capture offered by *converso* creationists, two key questions arise: What sense of the public interest should inform the humanities? And what should be their focus? The answers may come from Wilby's quotation in the first epigraph, which appeared in the *New Statesman* fifty years after Snow's original column: media and cultural studies. But those fields face insistent skepticism about Humanities Two overriding its other, per the DeLillo epigraph from *White Noise* and Goldberg's account of the political economy.

If we look at the resistance to co-optation by creative-industries fantasists, we see that ea_spouse and her interlocutors in the gaming industry are not alone. The German cultural-policy advocacy group Kultur Macht Europa issued an instructive, sterling declaration following its Fourth Federal Congress on Cultural Policy in 2007 about protecting both cultural workers and proprietors under copyright and other laws and the need to ensure diverse media texts as well as infrastructure. Similar concerns animate the Jodhpur Initiative for Promoting Cultural Industries in the Asia-Pacific Region, adopted by twenty-eight countries (Jodhpur Initiatives 2005). Inspired by such counters to creative-industries discourse, we need to follow Vincent Mosco's reminder that once the utopic rhetoric of new communications technologies and cultural genres has played out, when a "mythic period" of alarm and fantasy has given way to banality and every move is neither hailed nor derided but silently normalized, real work must begin (2004: 19). Otherwise, we are left with "freedom to choose after all the major political, economic, and social decisions have already been made" (60). These areas of analysis are just as important as the apolitical, ahistorical tendencies that characterize creative industries and games analysis.[1]

In the 1960s, Hoggart posed the following question, even as he championed the expansion of cultural studies into the popular and the practical: "What is one to make of a medieval historian or classicist who finds nothing odd—that is, nothing to be made sense of, at the least, if not opposed—in the sight of one of his new graduates going without second thoughts into, say, advertising; or of a sociologist or statistician who will undertake consultant work without much questioning the implications of the uses to which his work is put?" (1973: 100). Thirty years later, the Reaganite Virginia Postrel wrote a *Wall Street Journal* op-ed welcoming cultural studies as "deeply threatening to traditional leftist views of commerce . . . lending support to the corporate enemy and even training graduate students who wind up doing market research" (1999: A18).[2] Her celebratory remark suggests that this time of turmoil is birthing both positive and negative outcomes, per the New Right of cultural studies examined in the previous chapter.

---

1 Albeit with notable exceptions (Mirrlees 2009; Consalvo 2006; Lenoir 2003).

2. True-believer creationists can hire her at http://www.leighbureau.com/speaker.asp?id=288.

I use "media and cultural studies" as a portmanteau term for research and teaching that cover a multitude of cultural and communications machines and processes. There is increasing overlap between these sectors, as black-box techniques and technologies, once set apart from audiences, become subject to public debate and utilization. Consumer electronics connect to information and communication technologies, and vice versa: Televisions resemble computers; books are read on telephones; newspapers are written through clouds; films are streamed via rental companies; and so on. Genres and gadgets that once were separate are linked. Hence the media segment. At the same time, the significance of culture has widened in terms of geography, demography, language, genre, and theory. Hence culture.

The push for the study of media texts that reflect issues of consequence to the broad population can be central to renewing the humanities. The historic task of history and literature, what Stuart Hall (2004) nominates as "a humane, critical discourse designed to deepen the social awareness of a wider readership," must be transferred to additional media forms and liberated from its banal reliance on aesthetic narcissism. At the same time, its remit must broaden beyond *representing* social life to *embodying* it, in recognition that culture is becoming yet more central to the everyday economy rather than simply reflecting and refracting it.

In order to understand the world and lead meaningful lives within it—as denizens, citizens, and workers—people must understand how the media function in the global and local context of demographic change because of their importance for the future of employment and knowledge. Just as the "Two Cultures" distinction no longer wraps us in protective wool separating art from science, so a cross-pollinating world disseminates information and entertainment from far afield, providing stories and conflicts that are the stuff of media production (and can incorporate approaches from Humanities One and Two).

I realize, following a compelling commentary by Stuart Cunningham (pers. comm., 2011), that this may come across as special pleading or an attempt "to reinstate an imperializing 'queen of the sciences' . . . a disciplinary takeover" that favors my side over the rest. But I view the issue differently: The advantage of incendiary work at a moment of crisis comes courtesy of a more comprehensive interdisciplinarity than we find in either Humanities One or Two, constructed from the two major influences of our day that touch on the field—namely, cultural change and media power. I'm in media and cultural studies because I think it's the future. I don't think it's the future because I'm in it.

We must operate along twin models of global and national relevance, with research and syllabi structured to reflect the multimedia future of our society and economy and the intertwined cultures of our population. Our professoriat must cover each region of the world, the major cultural groupings within the U.S. population, and all media forms. This is in keeping with the National Humanities Alliance calling for "strong communication and analytical skills . . . understanding of civic institutions . . . knowledge of world history and cultures . . . [and] multiple language proficiency" (2010: 4).

The data support this contention. Between 1980 and 1998, annual world exchange of electronic culture grew from $95 billion to $388 billion. In 2003, these areas accounted for 2.3 percent of GDP across Europe, to the tune of €654 billion—more than real estate, food, and drink, and equal to chemicals, plastics, and rubber. Price-WaterhouseCooper predicts 10 percent annual global growth. The Intellectual Property Association estimates that copyright and patents generate $360 billion a year in the United States, putting them ahead of aerospace, automobiles, and agriculture. In 2005, the U.S. cultural industries were worth $1.38 trillion—11.12 percent of GDP and 23.78 percent of growth in the economy. They employ 12 percent of the workforce, up from 5 percent a century ago. And exports are in the hundreds of billions (Miller 2009a; Siwek 2006; Dreher 2002; McChesney and Schiller 2002; United Nations Conference on Trade and Development 2004: 3; Commission of the European Communities 2006).

Put another way, the U.S. economy has been adjusting from a farming and manufacturing base to a cultural one, especially in foreign trade. It now makes and sells feelings, ideas, money, health, insurance, and law—niche forms of identity, a.k.a. culture. The trend is to harness the population's cultural skills to replace lost agricultural and manufacturing employment with jobs in music, theater, animation, recording, radio, TV, architecture, software, design, toys, books, sport, heritage, tourism, advertising, fashion, crafts, photography, games, and cinema (Towse 2002; United Nations Educational, Scientific and Cultural Organization 2002). The NGA argues that "innovative commercial businesses, non-profit institutions and independent artists have become necessary ingredients in a successful region's 'habitat'" (quoted in Tepper 2002: 159). The British Academy notes, "Whereas the dominant global industries of the past focused on manufacturing industry, the key corporations today are increasingly active in the fields of communications, information, entertainment, leisure" (2004: 14–16, 18–19).

Economically, the media are the leading edge of many industries; politically, they are central to democratic communication; and culturally, they incarnate social trends. The Social Science Research Council (SSRC) surveys the scene thus:

> Changes in the technologies and organizational structure of the media are transforming public life—in the U.S. and around the world. These changes affect not only the forms of delivery of media content—digital broadcasting, the Internet, and so on—but more fundamentally the ways in which we understand the world, communicate with each other, and participate in public life. Advances in digital technologies, the concentration of media ownership, the privatization of communications infrastructures, and the expansion of intellectual property regimes are underlying features of this transformation—both its causes and effects, and global in reach. What do these developments mean for a democratic society? What does a rich democratic culture look like under these conditions and how can we achieve it? (Social Science Research Council 2007)

Alongside political-economic shifts in the importance of the media (and well appreciated by the creative-industries push), a major change in global demography began in the 1960s. It has continued as a consequence of several factors: reforms to the international division of labor, as manufacturing left the Global North and subsistence agriculture was eroded in the South; population growth through public-health initiatives; increases in refugees following numerous conflicts among satellite states of the United States and the Soviet Union; transformations of these struggles into intra- and transnational violence when half the imperial couplet unraveled; the associated decline of state socialism and triumph of finance capital; vastly augmented human trafficking; the elevation of consumption as a site of social action and public policy; renegotiation of the 1940s–1970s compact across the West between capital, labor, and government, reversing that period's redistribution of wealth downward; deregulation of key sectors of the economy; the revival of Islam and Christianity as transnational religious and political projects; and the development of civil-rights and social-movement discourses and institutions, extending cultural difference from tolerating the aberrant to querying the normal, then commodifying and governing the result.

Of the approximately 200 sovereign states in the world, more than 160 are culturally heterogeneous across five thousand ethnic groups. Between 10 and 20 percent of the world's population currently belongs to a racial and linguistic minority in their country of residence, and 900 million people affiliate with groups that suffer systematic discrimination. Perhaps three-quarters of the world system sees politically active minorities, and there are more than two hundred movements for self-determination across almost a hundred states (Miller 2007b).

There are now five key zones of immigration—North America, Europe, the Western Pacific, the Southern Cone, and the Persian Gulf—and five key categories of immigration: international refugees, internally displaced people, voluntary migrants, the enslaved, and the smuggled. The number of refugees and asylum seekers at the beginning of the twenty-first century was 21.5 million—three times the figure twenty years earlier. The International Organization for Migration estimates that global migration increased from 75 million to 150 million people between 1965 and 2000, and the United Nations reports that 2 percent of all people spent 2001 outside their region of birth, more than at any other moment in history. Migration has doubled since the 1970s, and the European Union has seen arrivals from beyond its borders grow by 75 percent in the last quarter century (Miller 2007d). By 2011, international migrants numbered approximately 214 million, or 3.1 percent of the global population; 27.1 million were unwillingly displaced from their home countries, up from 21 million in 2000 (International Organization for Migration, n.d.).

Whether voluntary or imposed, temporary or permanent, this mobility is accelerating. Along with new forms of communication, it enables unprecedented cultural displacement, renewal, and creation between and across origins and destinations. Most of these exchanges are structured in dominance: the majority of international investment and trade takes place within the Global North, while the majority of immigration is from the Global South. In response, we see simultaneous tendencies toward open and closed borders. Opinion polling suggests that sizable majorities across the world believe their national ways of life are threatened by global flows of people and things. In other words, their cultures appear to be under threat. At the same time, they feel unable to control their individual destinies. In other words, their subjectivities are under threat. So they oppose immigration, largely because of fear. No major recipient of migrants has ratified the United Nations' International Convention on the Protection of the Rights of All Migrant Workers and Members of Their Families, even though these countries benefit economically and culturally from those arrivals (Miller 2010b).

The contemporary period has witnessed many outbursts of regressive nationalism, whether via the belligerence of the United States, the anti-immigrant stance of Western Europe, or the crackdown on minorities in Eastern and Central Europe, Asia, and the Arab world. The populist outcome is often violent, resulting, for example, in race riots across thirty British cities in the 1980s; pogroms against Roma and migrant workers in Germany in the 1990s and Spain in 2000; the Palestinian intifadas of 1987–1993 and 2000–2005; migrant worker and youth struggles in France in 1990 and 2005; and in 2011, the Arab Spring, Spain and Greece's *indignados*, and the "Occupy" movements. Virtually any arrival can be racialized, especially if expatriates from former colonies. The two most significant sites of migration from the Global South to the North—Turkey and Mexico—see state and vigilante violence alongside corporate embrace in host countries.

In the United States, the first great wave of immigration left the country 87 percent European American, a proportion that remained static thanks to racialized immigration laws and policies up to 1965. The twentieth century saw the population grow by 250 percent (the equivalent figures are less than 60 percent for both France and Britain). In the past decade, the country's Asian and Pacific Islanders and Latin@s increased by 43 percent. Between those two groups, African Americans, and Native Americans, about a hundred million U.S. residents can now define themselves as minorities. Latin@s and Asians in the United States are proliferating at ten times the rate of Euro descendants, such that the proportion of white Americans is down to 64 percent of the population and projected to be 53 percent in 2050. The foreign-born segment of the country is 34 million—double the proportion in 1970 and half as many again as 1995—and immigration across the 1990s was up 37.7 percent on the previous decade. Almost half the people living in Los Angeles and Miami were born outside the country (you go, LA), and Latin@s accounted for half the growth in the U.S. population between 2003 and 2004. Latin@ immigrants were also appearing in new sites, like Iowa and North Carolina. According to the 2010 Census, 50.5 million (or 16 percent of the total population) were Latin@, up from 13 percent in 2000. In 1960, one in seventeen workers in the labor force came from beyond the United States (mostly Europe). Today, the proportion is one in six, the majority being from Latin America and Asia. And the trend is accelerating. Between 1996 and 2000, immigrants constituted close to half the net increase in the labor force. Of course, these official figures do not disclose the full picture. It has been suggested that 9 million foreign citizens live here without immigration documents, and they are joined by 300,000 new arrivals annually. In addition, hybridity is increasingly the norm. In 1990, one in twenty-three U.S. marriages crossed race and ethnicity. In 2010, one in seven did so (Miller 2007b; United States Census Bureau 2011; Passel, Wang, and Taylor 2010). This makes people like me, who are concerned about white gringo masculinity's death throes, both relieved and anxious: relieved that its days of hegemony are numbered but anxious about those death throes.

Universities are being transformed by these trends. In the decade to 2008, the proportion of white college students dropped by 8.6 percent, though they remained the majority ethnic group. Latin@ numbers grew 5 percent annually; African American, 4 percent; and Asian American, 3 percent (Desrochers, Lenihan, and Wellman 2010). The humanities have responded to these developments via an unsteady if understandable oscillation between being "cultural gatecrashers and agents of radical social change or cultural gatekeepers and champions of tradition" (Early 2009: 52).

The drive to change the curriculum has come from students as much as faculty, because demographic and hence cultural shifts are far in advance of the ethnic whiteness and monolingualism that still characterize our professoriat. The so-called culture wars of the 1980s and 1990s essentially turned on this debate: "Universities have finally had to deal with non-Western societies, with the literature, history, and particular concerns of women, various nationalities, and minorities; and with unconventional, hitherto untaught subjects such as popular culture, mass communications and film, and oral history." Edward Said was eighty years out of date in 1994 when he referred to the latter as "hitherto untaught subjects." This is not surprising. According to the traditions of Humanities One, the Ivy League that propelled him to prominence and kept him there was slow to acknowledge such topics. Said was right, however, to refer to the proliferation of courses touching on "issues like race, gender, imperialism, war, and slavery" as an "almost Copernican change in the general intellectual consciousness." Such changes shared the sense that the university was less removed from society than before—that it was subject to "a new worldliness." Meanwhile, defenders of a stately removal based on the "great books" tradition were happily cashing checks from coin-operated think tanks (1994: 2, 4–5).

These media and population trends are signs that the humanities can have their day in the sun. Culture is crucial to both advanced and developing economies. It provides the legitimizing ground for states and interest groups (such as African Americans, gays and lesbians, people who are hearing impaired, or evangelical Protestants) to claim resources and seek control of national narratives (Yúdice 1990). Whereas rights to culture did not appear in many constitutions until well into the twentieth century, contemporary charters emphasize culture again and again. The meaning is generally a double one, blending artistry and ethnicity, with implications for both aesthetic and social hierarchies. Culture comes to "regulate and structure . . . individual and collective lives" (Parekh 2000: 143) in competitive ways that harness art and collective meaning for political and commercial purposes. So the Spanish minister for culture addressed São Paolo's 2004 World Cultural Forum with a message of cultural maintenance that was about economic development *and* the preservation of identity—a means of economic and social growth and citizenship, understood as a universal value placed in the specificity of different cultural backgrounds ("Ministra española" 2004).

This is not some teleologically unfurling tale of progress toward integration. Rather, culture is a site of contestation, per the civil rights movement, opposition to the American War in Viet Nam, youth rebellion, China's Cultural Revolution, and Third-World resistance to multinational corporations (D. Schiller 2007: 19). Critics of cultural imperialism and colonialism such as Aimé Césaire, Amilcar Cabral, Frantz Fanon, Armand Mattelart, Herbert I. Schiller, and Ariel Dorfman have animated generations of scholarship on these topics. The heritage of this history is mapped in Figure 4.1, a model I have adopted from one developed by Richard Maxwell (2000).

In Maxwell's (2002) words, the task today is to "link a critique of neo-liberalism and a cultural studies approach to consumption . . . not by issuing nostrums against the pleasures of shopping but by paying attention to the politics of resource allocation that brings a consumption infrastructure into the built environment." Arvind Rajagopal notes that because television, the telephone, the Internet, and the neoliberal are all new to India, "markets and media generate new kinds of rights and new kinds of imagination . . . novel ways of exercising citizenship rights and conceiving politics" (2002: 65). For Rosalía Winocur, radio in Latin America since the fall of U.S.-backed dictatorships has offered a simultaneously individual and social forum for new expressions of citizenship in the context of de-centered politics, emergent identities, minority rights, and gender issues. It provides a public space that transcends old ideas subordinating difference and privileging elite experience (2002: 15, 91–93). Mosco starts from the power of cultural myths, then "builds a bridge to political economy" in his investigation of neoliberal *doxa* about empowerment, insisting on "the mutually constitutive relationship

	1950s	1960s	1970s	1980s	1990s	2000s	TODAY
Britain	Catalysts of British cultural studies: Edward Thompson, Raymond Williams, Richard Hoggart	CCCS (1964) Stuart Hall Althusser-inspired ideology and media Structuralism Articulation Gramscian work on hegemony					
France and Italy		Roland Barthes Umberto Eco Louis Althusser Michel Foucault					Feminist writers, critical analysts of race, fieldwork, and queer theory make advances in cultural studies
Africa		Frantz Fanon (Algeria) Amilcar Cabral (Guinea) National liberation as act of culture		Ngugi wa Thiong'o Ngugi wa Mirii (Kenya) Media studies (South Africa)			
Europe				Critical race/gender studies Ethnographic study of audiences Ien Ang Charlotte Brunsdon Dick Hebdige			United States, Canada, South Africa, and Australia enjoy growing student demand for popular culture studies; associations form
Australia				Cultural policy studies: Stuart Cunningham, Tom O'Regan, Tony Bennett			
Latin America		New Latin American cinema	Transregional socialism Chilean socialism Liberation pedagogy and psychology Ignacio Martín-Baró Paolo Freire	Jesús Martín-Barbero: Enculturation, mediation, mestizaje Néstor García Cancini: Hybridity	Cultural studies of the Americas	George Yúdice	Cultural policy studies and creative industries studies emerge
USA			Paddy Whannel Lawrence Grossberg Foucault-inspired work on discourse and micropolitics Performative theory	John Fiske: Polysemy, intertextuality, textual pleasure, resistance	Judith Butler	History: Robin Kelly	

Figure 4.1 Mapping the History of Cultural Studies

between political economy and cultural studies" as each mounts "a critique of the other" (2004: 6–7).

Across Latin America, media and cultural studies have adopted a more critical cultural focus than creative-industries discourse, per the Consejo Latinoamericano de Ciencias Sociales (Costa, Silveira, and Sommer 2003). Cultural studies at the Universidad Nacional Costa Rica offers a trans–Central American perspective on cultural change through the media (http://www.una.ac.cr). Ecuador's Universidad Andina Simón Bolívar focuses on cultural analysis and production through lenses of subalternity, transterritoriality, and local social identities, with an emphasis on cultural policy (http://www.uasb .edu.ec). Many scholars and activists committed to critical cultural-policy studies, such as Yúdice (2002) in Miami and Costa Rica; Stefano Harney (2002, 2010) in London; David Bell (2007), Kate Oakley (2004, 2006, in press), and David Hesmondhalgh in Leeds (2008); Geert Lovink in Amsterdam and Ned Rossiter in Sydney (Lovink and Rossiter 2007); Justin Lewis and his collaborators in Cardiff (Lewis, Inthorn, and Wahl-Jorgensen 2005); and Néstor García Canclini and Eduardo Nivón in Mexico City, beaver away, weathering slings and arrows from the comfortably pure ultra-left for engaging with commerce and the state, and sending a few of their own toward those who unproblematically embrace such links.

But the way these influences have functioned on the ground in the United States has not, by and large, been very profound. The humanities have veered between formalism and contextualism without blending them. Consider literary studies. As we have seen, it is the implicit price inflator and deflator of Humanities One due to its unsteady, unworthy status as the custodian of "Western Civilization." Undergraduate and graduate students and professors in literature generally inhabit and leave the university knowing how to analyze fictional texts in a formal and social way. But they are typically ignorant of where those texts physically come from or end up and what happened to them in between.

For example, who among us knows the number of books sold in the countries they study; how many people buy or borrow books each year and what proportion read virtual or material versions; which companies dominate publishing and why; how many publishers there are now versus ten or twenty years ago; or why the market for works of literary theory is shrinking? Can we explain the business structure of the industry; the experience of working in it as a forester, editor, or driver; the relationships of novelists, agents, and editors; or how books appear in the front of chain stores (or are never in stock)?

What about describing the role of the International Publishers Association (http://internationalpublishers.org), the Pan African Booksellers Association (http://www.panafricanbooksellersassocia tion.org), the Book Industry Study Group (http://www.bisg.org), the Publishers Database for Responsible Environmental Paper Sourcing (http://prepsgroup.com), the Federation of Indian Publishers (http:// fipindia.org), the Federation of European Publishers (http://fep-fee .be), the Society of Publishers in Asia (http://sopasia.com), or the Book Industry Environmental Council (http://bookcouncil.org)? Are classes being taught about the DMCA jeopardizing fair use by turning digital works into commodity forms and criminalizing their appropri- ation? Or criminalizing what the International Federation of Repro- duction Rights Organisations (http://ifrro.org) does? Do we know how the industry manages innovation and experimentation (Healy 2008)?

What kind of curriculum should replace the banal Arnoldian training of Humanities One and the supine vocational training of Humanities Two and the creative industries? What can substitute for nostalgic class parthenogenesis and instrumental conservatory in- struction? A third form must come from a blend of political economy, textual analysis, ethnography, and environmental studies such that students learn the materiality of how meaning is made, conveyed, and discarded.

Roger Chartier (1989) and Pierre Macherey (1977) offer programs for the humanities that problematize business as usual. They suggest that the study of meaning must take account of linguistic transla- tions, material publications, promotional paratexts, archival categori- zations, and the like—a historicized and spatial approach that focuses on conditions of existence. Texts accrete and attenuate meanings on their travels as they rub up against, trope, and are troped by other fic- tional and factual texts, social relations, and material objects, and as they are interpreted—all those moments that allow them to become, for example, "the literary thing" (Macherey 2007).

Such an approach fruitfully connects the study of culture to what Ian Hunter calls an "occasion . . . the practical circumstances governing the composition and reception of a piece" (1988a: 215) in accordance with Alec McHoul and Tom O'Regan's "discursive analysis of particular actor networks, technologies of textual exchange, circuits of communicational and textual effectivity, traditions of exegesis, commentary and critical practice" (1992: 5–6). This links to the model of sender-message-receiver developed within mathematics and communications (Weaver and Shannon 1963) and media and cultural studies' concern with the encoding and decoding of information (Eco 1972). In a similar vein, there is much to be gained from actor-network theory in tracking the career of globally circulating texts. Bruno Latour (1993) and his followers analyze cars, missiles, trains, enzymes, and research articles by allocating equal and overlapping significance to natural phenomena, social forces, and textual production. This is the "cultural science" of which Stephen Muecke has written so evocatively, "diplomatically engaging with all the human and non-human things in the ecology" (2009: 408).

I also find useful the way that García Canclini (2004) seeks an alternative to the nativism of yanqui discourse via what is referred to in Latin America as interculturalism. This transcends the hardy humanities perennial of ethical incompleteness delivered via multiculturalism and postcolonialism. García Canclini demonstrates that accounts of culture must engage with three key factors. First, there is a paradox: Globalization also deglobalizes, in that its dynamic and impact are not only about mobility and exchange but also about disconnectedness and exclusion. Second, minorities no longer primarily exist within nations—rather, they emerge at transnational levels as a result of massive migration by people who share languages and continue to communicate, work, and consume through them. Third, *demographic* minorities within sovereign states may not form *cultural* minorities, because majoritarian elites in one nation often dispatch their culture to another where they are an ethnic minority. In any search for a "common culture," the risk is totalitarianism (Frow 1999) unless commonality refers to a metacultural concept that is rooted in the negotiation of cultural difference and sameness and opposed to a privileged unity (which generally means some form of exclusionary nationalism).

The fundamental message I take from these models is this: Understanding culture requires studying it up, down, and sideways, in accord with Laura Nader's (1972) renowned call for an ethnography of the powerful rather than the oppressed and George Marcus's (1995) endorsement of multisited analysis that focuses on where cultural meaning begins, lives, and expires. That means knowing which companies make texts, physical processes of production and distribution, systems of cross-subsidy and monopoly profit making, the complicity of educational canons with multinational corporations' business plans, and press coverage, inter alia.

Put another way, if the humanities are primarily concerned with explaining how meaning is made, they must consider the wider political economy, and not simply in terms of culture as a reflective or refractive index of it but as *part of* that economy, because culture is the creature, inter alia, of "corporations, advertising, government, subsidies, corruption, financial speculation, and oligopoly" (McChesney 2009: 109).

Changing the current *doxa* of the humanities in this direction could enrich students' and professors' knowledge base, increase their means of intervention in cultural production, counter charges of social and commercial irrelevance, challenge the safe houses of interdisciplinarity and disciplinarity, and make the field's citizenship and social-movement claims more credible. That would mean abandoning history and literature as core nodes of the humanities, turning instead to the study of media and culture—a necessity recognized even by lovers of literary critique who acknowledge that older forms can spring from and into emergent nodes (Woodward 2009).

So let's reconsider cultural studies. At its best, cultural studies blends and blurs textual analysis of the popular with social theory and materialism, focusing on the margins of power rather than reproducing established lines of force and authority. In place of concentrating on canonical works of art, governmental leadership, or quantitative social data, cultural studies devotes time to subcultures, popular media, music, clothing, and sport. By looking at how culture is used and transformed by "ordinary" and "marginal" social groups, cultural studies sees people not simply as consumers but as potential producers of new social values and cultural languages. This amounts to a comprehensive challenge to academic business as usual. The investment in the popular makes waves in the extramural world, too, as the humanities' historic task of criticizing entertainment is sidestepped. In fact, new commercial trends become part of cultural studies itself. There are costs as well as benefits to this, as the previous chapter showed.

Cultural studies is a tendency across disciplines rather than a discipline itself. This is evident in practitioners' simultaneously expressed desires to refuse definition, insist on differentiation, and sustain conventional departmental credentials (as well as pyrotechnic, polymathematical capacities for reasoning and research). Cultural studies' continuities come from shared concerns and methods. The concern is the reproduction of culture through structural determinations on subjects versus their own agency, and the method is historical materialism. This distinguishes the tendency I favor from the New Right of cultural studies that parlays the gospel of creative industries.

Cultural studies must be animated by subjectivity and power—how human subjects are formed and experience cultural and social space. It takes its agenda and mode of analysis from economics, politics, media and communication studies, sociology, literature, education, the law, science and technology studies, environmentalism, anthropology, and history. The focus is gender, race, class, and sexuality in everyday life, under the sign of a commitment to progressive social change.

We can specify a desirable cultural studies as a mixture of economics, politics, textual analysis, gender theory, ethnography, history, postcolonial theory, material objects, and policy, animated by a desire to reveal and transform those who control the means of communication and culture and undertaken with constant vigilance over one's raison d'être and modus operandi. So at the same time as categorical devices from the social sciences are deployed as grids of investigation, their status as machines obliterating difference is brought into question. The result can be a productive intellectual polyphony that draws out contradiction and dissonance.

I recall my excitement when I first saw the front cover of the Birmingham Centre's *Working Papers in Cultural Studies 4* of 1973. Alongside a bricolage graphic of a thoughtful cherub, some compass points with dollar and pound signs, and a few printers' codes, the bottom center-left looked like this:

LITERATURE~SOCIETY
MOTOR RACING

It may seem natural for these topics to be together (as is the case in newspapers). But it is not academically "normal." To make them syntagmatic was *utterly sensible* in terms of people's lives and mediated realities and *utterly improbable* in terms of intellectual divisions of labor and hierarchies of discrimination. Bravo.

Of course, this new positioning of media and cultural studies will encounter hostility, as most hybrids do (see discussion of Leviticus in Douglas 1966). Hybrids disturb people, so we should expect this reaction. Some interdisciplinary history can help explain where we stand, how we got there, and what the likely reception will be to the changes I am proposing.

Media and cultural studies in the United States derive from three principal domains: communication, literary, and area studies. The communication studies domain had two major influences: British cultural studies as it was once located at the University of Birmingham and the Open University, which looked at issues of national culture through the lens of class, race, and gender and drew on Marxism and ethnographic and textual methods, and the anti-Marxist ritualistic and economic-historical approach associated with the University of Illinois. Literary studies mobilized in Romance language departments and English, focusing on film and multiculturalism. Within area studies, the main influence came from Latin America through media ethnography and urban anthropology. One can see the impact of these forces within such areas as American and ethnic studies. This heritage largely applies to Humanities One at fancy schools.

On the media front, speech communication emerged in the early twentieth-century United States to help white non-English-speaking migrants assimilate into the workforce. It became the first home of media education, because the engineering professors who founded radio stations in colleges during the 1920s needed program content and drew volunteers from that area after being rebuffed by literature mavens.

These stations doubled as laboratories, with research undertaken into technology, content, and reception. At the same time, schools of journalism were forming to produce newspaper workers (Kittross 1999). Mass communication emerged schizophrenically to criticize the media as forms of leftist propaganda and admire them as forms of advertising and national identity. This heritage largely applies to Humanities Two, to large state schools that are not Research One institutions.

These simultaneously practical and political origins have made media and cultural studies poor cousins of hitherto-central humanities fields like literature and history, especially at little liberal arts colleges and private Research One universities. So Robert W. McChesney laments that the study of the media is "regarded by the pooh-bahs in history, political science, and sociology as having roughly the same intellectual merit as, say, driver education" (2007: 16; also see Hilmes 2005: 113). Many people deride cultural studies as "a looming, lightning-filled, thunderhead" of people who "have never been swept off their feet by a line of verse" and wrongly believe they can change the social order through revised canons of content and interpretation (Rorty 1994: 579–80). The National Association of Scholars recently issued a report titled *The Vanishing West*, which surveyed undergraduate classes at top-ranked universities and found a fifty-year decline in classes on "*Western Civilization*" in favor of "an all-things-to-all-people cornucopia" (Ricketts et al. 2011; Kiley 2011). Of course, similar wailings could be heard decades ago from prophets of gloom who believed that "the old unity has disappeared" as a consequence of "new departments and courses, with conflicting aims and points of view" (Wooster 1932: 373).

Identical attitudes are expressed by the bourgeois yanqui media and many business leeches. The *Village Voice* dubs media and cultural studies "the ultimate capitulation to the MTV mind . . . couchpotatodom writ large. . . . [J]ust as Milton doesn't belong in the rave scene, sitcoms don't belong in the canon or the classroom" (Vincent 2000). Steve Forbes rages in his family zine against "the political correctness that stifles the genuine free flow of discussion and debate in so many higher-ed institutions." He predicts a future with "fewer ridiculous basket-weaving-like courses" (2011). On the left, *Dissent* hopes we are dying out:

The lack of seriousness that had been synonymous with the nineties—the intellectual fads, the pop culture studies, the French theories . . . collapsed under the weight of an economic meltdown. What once appeared to be a liberating application of high theory to essential aspects of political and cultural experience now seems silly. Tenured radicals have awakened out of their comfortable nineties slumber to reckon with full-scale catastrophe. (Mattson 2011)

Thanks for that.

Britain shows similar tendencies. It may provide hints about our future, because media and cultural studies have taken greater formal hold of the undergraduate curriculum there and drawn fire from almost every vantage point. For the *Times Literary Supplement*, media and cultural studies form the "politico-intellectual junkyard of the Western world" (Minogue 1994: 27). Pet Tory philosopher Roger Scruton (also a visiting scholar at the American Enterprise Institute) denounces us as "sub-Marxist gobbledook [*sic*]" (quoted in Beckett 2004). Fresh from winning the Man Booker Prize for Fiction, Howard Jacobson (2010) thundered that "if you can read media studies at university—anything that needs a 'studies' to validate it should be viewed with suspicion—then universities have forgotten their function," which is "to minister to civilisation." Britain's former inspector of schools denounces media studies as "a subject with little intellectual coherence and meager relevance to the world of work" (Woodhead 2009: 9). On the left, the International Socialists bemoan that media and cultural studies devalue aesthetics, which supposedly denies the proletariat access to avant-garde and bourgeois art (Molyneux 2010). For Frank Kermode, the institutionalization of cultural studies "has resulted in new, self-perpetuating university departments and has packed existing departments with sympathizers" rather than focusing on "fine things" and "sane people" (1997).

Critics hold us "responsible for everything from undergraduates arriving at university unable to write proper sentences to the precipitous decline in the numbers taking Latin and Greek. No subject is the focus of so much sneering" (Morrison 2008: 8). Cambridge, for example, derides us *tout court*, while Antony Beevor advised the *Guardian*'s

Hay Festival of Books that "media studies is seen as a bad joke as far as employers are concerned." Such "soft subjects" amount to "a betrayal of the students," who "have been conned" (quoted in Higgins 2010).

In 2011, the leading group of U.K. universities issued a formal warning to school pupils that "the optimum nutrition for the formation of buoyant little grey cells is science and maths, alongside portions of history, geography and languages, dead or alive." Media and cultural studies deliver "empty carbs" (Friedberg 2011) in part because they are "vocational or have a practical bias" and are hence "soft" (quoted in Shepherd 2011). The Media Education Association retorted that students in these areas "are required to master complex theories relating to topics such as identity, representation and ideology, and to understand the workings of powerful media institutions and practitioners" (McDougall and Bazalgette 2011).

The *Observer* scornfully mocks us with a parental parody: "What better way to have our little work-shy scholars rushing off to read an improving book than to enthuse loudly in their presence about how the omnibus edition of *EastEnders* [1985–, a soap opera] is the new double physics?" (Hogan 2004). Britain's *Telegraph* derides media studies as "quasi-academic" (Lightfoot 2005; Paton 2007a) and deliciously quotes a leaked government e-mail referring to "Mickey Mouse courses" such as "Third World Development with Pop Music" (Barrett, Malnick, and Buscombe 2010). The alarmingly Oedipal *Guardian* columnist Simon Hoggart could be seen on British television in 2000 chiding local universities for wasting time on this nonsense when they should be in step with Harvard and MIT. Chris Patten, a former Conservative Party politician, the last governor of Hong Kong, current chancellor of Oxford, and the chair of the BBC Trust, refers to the discipline as "Disneyland for the weaker minded" (quoted in Morley 2007: 17). Many critics question whether we offer "a Mickey Mouse degree, or a means to understand the cultural significance of Mickey Mouse" (Snowdon 2010)—and what the difference might be. Both the ruling Conservative Party and Alan Sugar, U.K. inquisitor for *The Apprentice* (2005–), worry that media studies "may be putting future scientific and medical innovation under threat" and "undermining the economy" (Paton 2007b, 2008). In Australia, where some media courses are difficult to get into and require high entry scores, reactionaries decry the area as obscurantist, "degenerate" (a wonderful term), and misleading, because it supposedly attracts students through vocationalism while lacking articulations to industry (Windschuttle 2006).

Most of all, media and cultural studies' popularity with British students (in 1997, thirty-one thousand English school pupils took it; in 2008, the number was fifty-eight thousand) irritates right-wing anti-intellectuals in the media (Morrison 2008; Ellis 2005). Such critics favor market-based education derived from preferences—other than when they lead people to learn about the media! At the same time, the U.K. government claims that Britain "leads the way worldwide in the study of media-related subjects, and is highly respected" (British Council 2006: 1). Chinese students flock there to take these classes, which are lacking at home and are seen as more practical than traditional information-technology courses because they emphasize texts rather than wires, meaning rather than manufacture (Hodges 2009).

So we see media and cultural studies being simultaneously more vocational than many other subjects, thanks to a commitment to production skills, drama, and news-and-current affairs research; more populist, given its legitimization of the everyday and success with students; and more politicized, because of the British tradition's imprint of leftism and feminism (Turner 2007).

It is worth recalling that new subject areas always cause controversy when they enter universities. This was the British experience with the introduction of the natural sciences in the nineteenth century and politics, philosophy, English, and sociology in the twentieth. We have already seen how literature displaced classics in the United States. These were practical responses to major socioeconomic transformations—industrialization, state schooling, class mobility, and public welfare (Fox 2003; Whittam Smith 2008). Many of the claims made against our work are as silly as critiques of those earlier developments. Foucault rightly proposes that we think of the media on a continuum with universities, journals of tendency, and books—each one is a medium, and it is strange to treat one or the other as more or less significant or powerful as a venue or topic (2001: 928).

The British Academy has recognized a foundational concern with justice and equality in its support for interdisciplinary work on culture that enables "disadvantaged and marginalized people and communities to find new means of expression." It is also evident in cultural studies' role as a site for blending humanities and social science approaches to such issues as migration and gender (2004: 6, 11, 45). This is about applied activism, just like the labors of engaged intellectuals in civil engineering, economic advice, social welfare, pharmaceutical development, contract law, or public policy, with commitments to social and cultural stakeholders as well as disciplinary gatekeepers and rent seekers (Costa, Silveira, and Sommer 2003).

Only an Olympian self-satisfaction could assert that citizenship roles for the humanities belong "to an earlier period" and lack "cash value," that claims for their contribution to economic development are spurious: "Nobody really buys that argument, not even the university administrators who make it" (Fish 2008b, 2010a). That is patently absurd if you peek at media studies, creative writing, public speaking, film schools, and so on and you have the ken to understand shifts in the wider political economy. I meet both government and corporate people who read our work. They may dislike the politics, but they use the facts and analysis because we do more than reinterpret adored words and images for the purpose of aesthetic self-formation (though we like that, too, and see it as worth undertaking as well as interrogating).

New forms of humanities education are required that combine media and cultural theory and practice via innovations that disobey traditional disciplinary divisions and cross the pathways of cultural production, interpretation, and power. Multimedia design, copyright law, narrative systems, environmental impact, and global flows of people, money, and culture must become part of students' knowledge. The twenty-first-century Literacy Summit noted that even as key channels of cultural distribution are increasingly corporate, governmental, and narrow, the capacity to make and distribute stories and facts through the media is available as never before. In 1999, Atlantic Philanthropies funded a multiyear, multimillion-dollar study of how the media are changing curricular and research agendas as new producers and audiences emerge. Similar experiments are happening across the United States, such as the James Irvine Foundation's Communities Organizing to Advance Learning Initiative (New Media Consortium 2005: 2–3, 6, 8).

This necessitates what is called in the academic literature on innovation "3rd generation work" ("1st generation" refers to traditional disciplinary policing, "2nd generation" to collaboration across traditional disciplines, and "3rd generation" to somewhere beyond them). It is the direction favored by the Council of Europe, the Organisation for Economic Co-operation and Development (OECD), UNESCO, and the European Union (Metcalfe et al. 2006: 17, 49). Study after study, from the Association of American Universities; the American Council on Education; the Committee on Science, Engineering, and Public Policy; the NRC; the Sloan Foundation; and the Council of Graduate Schools, underscores the need for interdisciplinarity at the core of universities, as embodied in the NRC's panels on national doctoral education. The NSF's Integrative Graduate Education and Research Traineeship scheme was designed to break through the limits of nineteenth- and early mid-twentieth-century disciplines by permitting scientists and engineers to undertake interdisciplinary doctorates, "stimulating collaborative research that transcends traditional disciplinary boundaries" (Nyquist and Wulff 2000; also see Woodrow Wilson National Fellowship Foundation 2004; and Ostriker and Kuh, with Voytuk 2003).

The ACLS Commission on Cyberinfrastructure for the Humanities and Social Sciences acknowledges the blurring of boundaries created by the spread of information and interpretation through new cultural technologies. It calls for interdisciplinarity to develop, maintain, recover, and distribute what it calls the "cultural commonwealth" (2006). This is no cybertarian faith in social networks offering new forms of communication but a considered and weighty history of pedagogical investigation animated by new prospects. As we have seen, universities like "new" media such as electronic games, thanks to their applications to militarism and Mammon through governmental and commercial fetishes for new technology. In the words of the ACLS, "What we once called 'film studies' increasingly will be research on digital media" (Yu 2006: ii). We should welcome aspects of this development, even as we are alert to the excesses outlined in the previous chapter.

The future of the humanities does not lie in the autonomy of scholarship and culture. It is about thriving in the context of difference and economic change, in ways that make us fit for purpose and progressive. Media and cultural studies are well placed to be cornerstones of this new work because they are both disciplinary and interdisciplinary formations and dynamic challenges to the status quo yet interested and invested in commercial culture (Turner 2012). Such forms of engagement are required alongside a fervent push for a renewed humanities to take its place at the public-policy table.

Conclusion

How can Obama save our economy and our democracy? Humanities education.
    —Danny Heitman, "How Can Obama Save Our Economy and Our Democracy?"

Many in the humanities have accepted demands to provide a particular kind of serviceability to business and the economy. Some can even be heard spouting the ideology of efficiency, productivity and utility, which are profoundly not conducive to our intellectual discipline. A negative politics that claims that researchers in the humanities produce cold facts out of a hat with as much cunning and cleverness as any white-cloaked scientist, or that we write as "disembodied observers" of objective truths, leaves us with no room for anything save the paradox of purchasing our intellectual freedom through self-immolation.
    —Joanna Bourke, "Humanities Need to Get Off the Back Foot"

Most people feel secure within the narrow confines and well-trodden paths of their own upbringing . . . time-honoured yet segregated playgrounds for discovery and interpretation.
    —Malcolm Gillies, "Preface," in *Collaborating across the Sectors*

We often think of the U.S. research university as the peak of higher education. And so it is, if one focuses on inventions, prizes, salaries, libraries, citations, endowments, laboratories, and grants. But what about people who are not so much surfing this wave as being dumped by it? The current conjuncture of U.S. higher education is colored by crisis. The businesses and governments it seeks to serve and emulate are revealed to be naked and saggy, even as the promises of futurism appear deliverable only via the proletarianization of scholarly work. This is a turning point in educational history, with pages torn from a playbook and lives torn asunder. Dedicated researchers who join the ranks of the gentried poor rather than follow Mammon find that the supposed trade-off— pursuing research secure in the knowledge that their basic welfare is guaranteed—no longer applies. In its place comes a risky form of life that enables and indexes the information society's institutionalized deinstitutionalization. Yet Heitman (2011), writing in the *Christian Science Monitor*, among many others, regards the humanities— willful, inefficient, and cloistered though they may be—as the last chance for creating a concerned and aware citizenry. That leaves us with potential room to move.

This does not mean turning the clock back to a magical era that never existed. A tasteless but hitherto ineradicable binary of gringo humanities uplift contrasts "the hierarchical graces of Europe" with "the romantic vision of vanished America, rural, small-town, face-to-face"—something that never was versus something quickly lost (Miliband 1962: 16). It cloaks the humanities' service to money and militarism within a sheath of high versus popular culture. It is also not practical or desirable to flourish the credentials of a high-handed if heavy-hearted removal from the everyday. The evidence presented throughout this book illustrates that the humanities "need as many friends and links as possible" (Gillies 2009: 36). For example, I cannot afford to argue only to my fellow socialists.

Universities are what Foucault (1986a) called heterotopias—spaces where a better future can be represented. (*Heterotopia* is the nice word for "not the real world.") One move might be to take the heterotopia of the university as a desirable model for an equitable society rather than a laughable site of cloistered privilege. That would place a premium on inquiry and knowledge. Corporations would invest in more than immediate returns. Governance would be shared between employees, managers, and owners. And a green administration would urge innovative consumption as well as production. Inspiration in these directions comes from numerous quarters, notably the British *Manifesto for Higher Education* (2011).

Increases in governmentalization and commodification are necessary by-products of higher education as it expands to include more people, alongside transformations in the economy that center intellectual property. We should point out when and where those side effects are antidemocratic, but we cannot swim against a material tide other than by invoking an outmoded, exclusionary elitism. Hence the requirement to center the media in the new humanities: They are pivotal for citizenship, work, and consumption, as never before. This need not mean increased tuition or fiscal panic on the part of the state (Imre Szeman, pers. comm., 2011). Rather, it necessitates working to reverse a three-way shift in applied political-economic theory. That shift has lowered taxes on the wealthy, diminished block grants to higher education by governments, and mandated augmented expenditure by students. The first part of this tottering tripod is animated by the disproven fantasy of trickle-down economics. The second part assumes that artificially created markets for public goods create greater returns. And the third part argues that education should be freely provided only to children.

We must call for a comprehensive redefinition of the U.S. research effort so that it downplays useless knowledge and plays up useful knowledge. What does that mean? An adjustment away from the Cold War industrial categories that still define research policy. The few things we make in this benighted land that others want to buy include, most critically, services—which is to say, "culture" or "intellectual property." A major public-policy push toward renaming the NSF the National Research Foundation must accompany learning from the wacky folks over at creative industries as we sit down with scientists and social scientists to find common ground.

The old world of creating martial men/multicultural subjects has to give up its absurd claims to understanding the quintessence of humanity through a faulty anthropology that is scarred by origins in slavery, hypermasculinity, and Romantic philosophy. Great books that cultivate the soul buy into this myth—regardless, I'm sorry, of the race, gender, or politics of their authors. Such a process remains caught in a powerful but flawed dialectic that recenters again and again the authority of the professor in the name of ethically incomplete student subjects.

Even in the restricted definition of the NEA, "art works" refers, inter alia, to the fact that there were "two million full-time artists" and almost six million "arts-related jobs" in the United States in 2010 (Art Works, n.d.). If we return to the federal legislation that created the NEH and the NEA, the case made for the humanities was actually quite a good one. It offers the public "a better understanding of the past, a better analysis of the present, and a better view of the future." Put another way, "democracy demands wisdom and vision in its citizens." The law makes various high-minded remarks about aesthetics, as one might expect (National Foundation on the Arts and the Humanities Act of 1965). But its kernel lies in these statements.

Conversely, the Association of American Colleges and Universities (AACU) welcomes *Wired* magazine's promulgation in 2010 of a "Neoliberal Arts." The association proudly advises that *"Wired* Names the Neoliberal Arts—and They Look a Lot Like AAC&U's Essential Learning Outcomes" (Humphreys 2010). The "neoliberal arts" are described as "higher learning for highly evolved humans." This buys into two, seemingly contradictory, impulses. On the one hand, neoliberalism stands for an utterly depthless norm, where change, choice, chance, and competition are the vocabulary. Conversely, evolution, despite its mandate in change, is about very, very slow responsiveness to altered material circumstances. Not surprisingly, *Wired*'s curriculum is banally obvious. One for the ancients, it invokes statistics, diplomacy, culture, thought, communication, and nature, albeit with updated applications ("7 Essential Skills" 2010). The creative industries meet martial masculinity.

Although that option, too, is flawed, the push for something new simply has to be joined—and changed. The AACU states that "a consensus is emerging about the kind of education that Americans need to thrive in a knowledge-intensive economy, a globally engaged democracy, and a society where innovation is essential" (Humphreys 2010). Employers clearly indicate that they want college graduates, regardless of discipline, with knowledge of technology, cultural diversity, and globalization (Hart Research Associates 2010). *Forbes* magazine worries that state investment in apparently instrumental subjects such as engineering engages only half the needs of innovation and growth, because it ignores "creativity, artistry, intuition, symbology, fantasy, emotions." Snow's binary still holds. This bias must go, in favor of curricula designed to form "whole-brain scientists," unlike the narrow outcomes produced by NSF funding stimuli. Most engineers and technologists work outside academia and must hence function in mixed company, so their training should also be mixed, per liberal education (Mills and Ottino 2009).

And a 2011 poll indicates that while Congress favors cutting public expenditure on higher education by 26 percent and the White House seeks to increase it by 9 percent, the general public wants to double it, along with massive cuts to the Pentagon budget (Kull et al. 2011). The tremors that are undulating across corporate agendas and governmental methods may thereby enable us to combat them in the light of the remarkable achievements of *los indignados* and the "Occupy" movements. It is precious and trite for academicians to suggest that their agenda should be entirely separate from that of capital—and vice versa. So Harney (2010) argues for reversing the mimetic managerial fallacy with which I began. Working in a business school, he wants such entities to become more humanities-like, in the sense of adopting critical attitudes to justice and innovation.

We can shift the mimetic managerial fallacy into reverse by implementing collaborative (not competitive) and learned (not leeched) forms of work. Utilizing accountability to reveal corporate power over intellectual production, or pointing out to students the negative realities of a consumer address, can be fruitful. In accordance with the brave actions taken by anthropologists and psychologists against war, and scientists and novelists against war profiteering, we should shame universities for their role in militarism, even as we acknowledge that this has its origins in the crass commercialism of a system in crisis that feeds from the death roll of a discredited empire. The task is massive, and it will require people with progressive politics to collaborate as never before.

I suspect that the intellectual core across the two humanities is the struggle for meaning—how it is established and disestablished, and what it is. This is clearly central to historical interpretation, philosophical speculation, textual analysis, linguistic training, legal precedent, political theory, religious superstition, cultural production, and sociocultural organization (see Frow 2005). Synthesizing and highlighting these commonalities inside a more comprehensive and materialist method would equip our students for contemporary citizenship and work.

Here is the future for the humanities: comprehensive, omnibus survey courses about how meaning is made, circulated, and received in all media—running across science, capital, fiction, sport, news, history, and politics. That means undertaking research into these topics and associated fields, with necessary foci on business, government, labor, and demography, which would break down the binarism of "great books courses" from "great issues courses," as part of dwelling in a networked, competitive, global labor market and citizen pool (Gillies 2009: 35).

We must get over the fact that collaborative work remains frowned on—or at least not understood—in the humanities, because that further entrenches our backwardness as we overcommit to the single-authored monograph's monastic model of knowledge and comprehensive lack of interdisciplinarity (Canadian Federation for the Humanities and Social Sciences 2006).

I am fortunate to have experienced a thorough interdisciplinarity. Before being disrupted by mimetic managerial bureaucrats, Griffith and Murdoch Universities in Australia were remarkable sites of teaching and research, founded on problem solving rather than scholarly specialization. I taught at both of them in their heydays, receiving a lot more than I gave.[1]

We worked in teams, so courses would quite naturally see collaborators whose knowledge arched across ethnomethodology, literary theory, political economy, public policy, communications, film studies, history, and philosophy. This was not the interdisciplinarity so often crowed about in the humanities—interdisciplinarity without multiple languages, numbers, ethnography, geography, environ-

---

1. This was also because of the conjuncture of expanding higher education, Keynesian economic policies, and remarkable people working in the cultural and media fields in Brisbane and Perth at those times. An indicative list includes Peter Anderson, Tony Bennett, Marion Campbell, Stuart Cunningham, John Darling, Michael Dutton, Rita Felski, John Fiske, John Frow, Mitzi Goldman, Melissa Harpley, John Hartley, Richard Higgott, Bob Hodge, Ian Hunter, Noel King, Niall Lucy, Alan Mansfield, Tony May, Alec McHoul, Jim McKay, Colin Mercer, Jeffrey Minson, Vijay Mishra, Albert Moran, Tom O'Regan, Richard Robison, Garry Rodan, Horst Ruthrof, David Saunders, Krishna Sen, Brian Shoesmith, Lesley Stern, Sally Stockbridge, Jon Stratton, Gordon Tait, Graeme Turner, Jon Watts, Gary Wickham, and Dugald Williamson. I learned something every day by being among them.

mentalism, or experiments. It was much more challenging. I have since worked with such models in research teams that have generated books, articles, journals, and seminars. They function best with young scholars who want to do something new rather than feather nests.

In the United States, the humanities' marginal status derives from the fact that we are regarded as "an ornament of society" (Gillies 2009: 37) while desiring to be its core. The economic reductionism abjured by the humanities is no longer a sustainable alibi for dodging the power and applicability of numbers and structures. The taste for interpretation, for single-text analysis, for the Romantic elevation of consciousness, for a hermeneutics of suspicion, for a notion of ethical incompleteness, remains vibrant, even foundational. As the object of analysis undergoes multiple transformations and becomes a force of material as much as symbolic power, attention must turn to theorizing the economy and its relations to culture.

Humanities One and Two must merge. They must learn from one another, with the philosophical ideas of One meeting the institutional ideas of Two. They must find common cause, then reach out to colleagues and fellow travelers in other parts of campus and the wider political economy, be they scientists, publishers, librarians, creationists, or gamers, be they precarious, tenured, or wonky. The centrality of a new, refurbished, collectivist humanities to rebalancing our economy and society must be asserted to all these players in a way that is credible to social movements, workers, and policy makers. To do otherwise would be to write the longest suicide note in history.

References

"AA:SF Tops 9 Million User Mark!" 2008. America's Army, February 10. Available at http://www.americasarmy.com/press/news.php?t=70.

"About *The Lancet* Medical Journal." n.d. TheLancet.com. Available at http://www.thelancet.com/lancet-about.

Ackerman, Spencer. 2010. "Pentagon's Purchasers Get Their Own Video Games." *Wired*, December 8. Available at http://www.wired.com/dangerroom/2010/12/pentagons-purchasers-get-their-own-video-games.

Adorno, Theodor W. 2009. "*Kultur* and Culture." Translated by Mark Kalbus. *Social Text* 99:145–58.

Agger, Ben, and Allan Rachlin. 1983. "Left-Wing Scholarship: Current Contradictions of Academic Production." *Humanities in Society* 6 (2–3): 241–56.

Albanese, Andrew. 2002. "PubSCIENCE Dies Despite Comments: Opponent SIIA Now Takes Aim at Two Other Free Public Databases." *Library Journal*, December 15, 17.

Alonso, Carlos J., Cathy N. Davidson, John M. Unsworth, and Lynne Withey. 2003. *Crises and Opportunities: The Futures of Scholarly Publishing*. Paper no. 57. New York: American Council of Learned Societies.

American Academy of Pediatrics, Council on Communications and Media. 2009. "Policy Statement—Media Violence." *Pediatrics* 124 (5): 1495–1503.

American Anthropological Association. 2006. "Anthropologists Weigh In on Iraq, Torture at Annual Meeting." December 11. Available at http://www.aaanet.org/pdf/iraqtorture.pdf.

American Behavioral Scientist. 2000. "Legitimacy in the Modern World," special issue, 43 (9): 1371–1560.

American Council of Learned Societies. 2012. "Frequently Asked Questions." Available at http://www.acls.org/info/Default.aspx?id=198.

American Council of Learned Societies Commission on Cyberinfrastructure for the Humanities and Social Sciences. 2006. *Our Cultural Commonwealth.* New York: American Council of Learned Societies.

American Economic Association. 2012. "The *American Economic Review*: Information for Reviewers." Available at http://www.aeaweb.org/aer/reviewers.php.

American Society for Cell Biology. 2007. "ASCB Position on Public Access to Scientific Literature." Available at http://www.ascb.org/files/policy/position_paper/ASCBPositionPaperonPublicAccesstotheScientificLiterature.pdf.

Andersen, Robin. 2007. "Bush's Fantasy Budget and the Military/Entertainment Complex." *PRWatch*, February 12. Available at http://prwatch.org/node/5742.

Anderson, Chris. 2007. "Are Dead-Tree Magazines Good or Bad for the Climate?" *Long Tail*, December 27. Available at http://longtail.com/the_long_tail/2007/12/are-dead-tree-m.html.

Arnold, Matthew. 1875. *Essays in Criticism.* 3rd ed. London: Macmillan.

Aronowitz, Stanley. 2000. *The Knowledge Factory: Dismantling the Corporate University and Creating True Higher Learning.* Boston: Beacon Press.

Art Works. n.d. "About Art Works." Available at http://www.arts.gov/artworks/?page_id=79. Accessed March 2, 2012.

Arts and Humanities Research Council. 2009. "Leading the World: The Economic Impact of UK Arts and Humanities Research." June 16. Available at http://www.ahrc.ac.uk/News/Latest/Pages/leadingtheworld.aspx.

———. 2010. "Impact Summary and Pathways to Impact Frequently Asked Questions—AHRC." Available at http://www.ahrc.ac.uk/FundingOpportunities/Documents/ImpactFAQ.pdf.

Association of American University Presses Task Force on Economic Models for Scholarly Publishing. 2011. *Sustaining Scholarly Publishing: New Business Models for University Presses.* New York: Association of American University Presses Task Force.

Association of Learned and Professional Society Publishers, European Association of Science Editors, and Academy of the Learned Societies for the Social Sciences. 2000. *Current Practice in Peer Review: Results of a Survey Conducted during Oct/Nov 2000.* Worthing, UK: Association of Learned and Professional Society Publishers.

Attali, Jacques. 2008. "This Is Not America's Final Crisis." *New Perspectives Quarterly* 25 (2): 31–33.

Augustine. 1976. *Concerning the City of God against the Pagans.* Edited by David Knowles. Translated by Henry Bettenson. Harmondsworth, UK: Penguin.

Australian Academy of the Humanities. 2010. *Submission in Response to Research Workforce Strategy Consultation Paper: Meeting Australia's Research Workforce Needs.* Available at http://www.innovation.gov.au/Research/ResearchWorkforceIssues/Documents/RWSsubmissions/Submission 68.pdf.

Ayers, Edward L. 2009. "Where the Humanities Are." *Daedalus* 138 (1): 24–34.

Bakhshi, Hasan, Philippe Schneider, and Christophe Walker. 2008. *Arts and Humanities Research and Innovation.* London: Arts and Humanities Research Council/National Endowment for Science, Technology and the Arts.

Bar, François, with Caroline Simard. 2006. "From Hierarchies to Network Firms." In *The Handbook of New Media: Updated Students Edition,* edited by Leah Lievrouw and Sonia Livingstone, 350–63. Thousand Oaks, CA: Sage.

Barrett, David, Edward Malnick, and Chris Buscombe. 2010. "Quango Opposes Crackdown on 'Mickey Mouse' Degrees." *The Telegraph,* September 5. Available at http://www.telegraph.co.uk/education/universityeducation/7981792/Quango-opposes-crackdown-on-Mickey-Mouse-degrees.html.

Barthes, Roland. 1984. *Image-Music-Text.* London: Fontana.

Bauerlein, Mark. 2006. "A Very Long Disengagement." *Chronicle of Higher Education,* January 6, B6–B8.

———. 2008. "The Future of Humanities Labor." *Academe Online,* September–October. Available at http://www.aaup.org/AAUP/pubsres/academe/2008/SO/Feat/baue.htm.

Beckett, Francis. 2004. "Bad Press, Good Press." *The Guardian,* January 19. Available at http://www.guardian.co.uk/education/2004/jan/20/higher education.mediastudiescommunicationsandlibrarianship.

Bedey, David F. 2008. "Exclusive: Higher Education and 'The Vacuity of Hope.'" *Family Security Matters,* June 20. Available at http://www.family securitymatters.org/publications/id.414,css.print/pub_detail.asp.

Bell, Daniel. 1977. "The Future World Disorder: The Structural Context of Crises." *Foreign Policy* 27:109–35.

Bell, David. 2007. "Fade to Grey: Some Reflections on Policy and Mundanity." *Environment and Planning A* 39 (3): 541–54.

Berrett, Dan. 2011a. "Humanities, for Sake of Humanity." *Inside Higher Ed,* March 30. Available at http://www.insidehighered.com/news/2011/03/30/scholars_seek_to_craft_argument_for_urgency_of_the_humanities_in_higher_education.

———. 2011b. "The 'Inside Job' Effect." *Inside Higher Ed,* April 19. Available at http://www.insidehighered.com/news/2011/04/19/economists_start_probing_their_own_ethics.

———. 2011c. "Yanked from the Margins." *Inside High Ed,* February 18. Available at http://www.insidehighered.com/news/2011/02/18/new_commission_to_advance_the_cause_of_the_humanities_and_social_science.

Bloom, Allan. 1974. "The Failure of the University." *Daedalus* 103 (4): 58–66.

Blumenstyk, Goldie. 2002. "Universities Try to Keep Inventions from Going 'out the Back Door.'" *Chronicle of Higher Education*, May 17, A33–34.

———. 2010. "Saving the Life of the Mind." *Chronicle of Higher Education*, February 28. Available at http://chronicle.com/article/Colleges-Transform-the-Liberal/64398.

Boffey, David. 2011. "Academic Fury over Order to Study the Big Society." *The Observer*, March 26. Available at http://www.guardian.co.uk/education/2011/mar/27/academic-study-big-society.

Bohannon, John. 2008. "'Spore' Documentary Spawns Protest by Scientists Who Starred in It." *Science* 322:517.

Bourke, Joanna. 2010. "Humanities Need to Get off the Back Foot." *The Guardian*, November 26. Available at http://www.guardian.co.uk/commentisfree/2010/nov/26/humanities-education.

Branin, Joseph J., and Mary Case. 1998. "Reforming Scholarly Publishing in the Sciences: A Librarian Perspective." *Notices of the American Mathematical Society* 45 (4): 475–86.

Brinkley, Alan. 2009. "The Landscape of Humanities Research and Funding." *Humanities Indicators Prototype*. Available at http://www.humanitiesindicators.org/essays/brinkley.pdf.

Brint, Steven G., Lori Turk-Bicakci, Kristopher Proctor, and Scott Patrick Murphy. 2009. "Expanding the Social Frame of Knowledge: Interdisciplinary, Degree-Granting Fields in American Colleges and Universities, 1975–2000." *Review of Higher Education* 32 (2): 155–83.

British Academy. 2004. *"That Full Complement of Riches": The Contributions of the Arts, Humanities and Social Sciences to the Nation's Wealth*. Available at http://www.britac.ac.uk/policy/full-complement-riches.cfm.

British Council. 2006. "Media Studies." Available at http://www.britishcouncil.org/learning-infosheets-media-studies.pdf.

Bromley, Carl. 1999. "What Hollywood Wants from Uncle Sam." *The Nation*, April 5, 28.

Brooks, Thom. 2011. "'Observergate' and Academic Freedom." *New Statesman*, April 15. Available at http://www.newstatesman.com/blogs/cultural-capital/2011/04/research-funding-ahrc-society.

Bruno, Isabelle, and Christopher Newfield. 2010. "Can the Cognitariat Speak?" *e-flux* 14 (3). Available at http://www.e-flux.com/journal/view/118.

Brzezinski, Zbigniew. 1969. *Between Two Ages: America's Role in the Technotronic Era*. New York: Viking Press.

Burston, Jonathan. 2003. "War and the Entertainment Industries: New Research Priorities in an Era of Cyber-Patriotism." In *War and the Media: Reporting Conflict 24/7*, edited by Daya Kishan Thussu and Des Freedman, 163–75. London: Sage.

Busch, Lawrence, Richard Allison, Craig Harris, Alan Rudy, Bradley T. Shaw, Toby Ten Eyck, Dawn Coppin, Jason Konefal, and Christopher Oliver, with

James Fairweather. 2004. *External Review of the Collaborative Research Agreement between Novartis Agricultural Discovery Institute, Inc. and the Regents of the University of California.* East Lansing: Institute for Food and Agricultural Standards, Michigan State University.

Cadin, Loïc, Francis Guérin, and Robert DeFillippi. 2006. "HRM Practices in the Video Game Industry: Industry or Country Contingent?" *European Management Journal* 24 (4): 288–98.

California Department of Education. 2011. "Textbook Weight in California." Available at http://cde.ca.gov/ci/cr/cf/txtbkwght.asp.

Canadian Federation for the Humanities and Social Sciences. 2006. *Large-Scale Research Projects and the Humanities.* Available at http://www.fedcan.ca/ftpFiles/documents/HumanitiesReportFinalEng.pdf.

Carley, Kathleen, Il-Chul Moon, Mike Schneider, and Oleg Shigiltchoff. 2005. *Detailed Analysis of Factors Affecting Team Success and Failure in the America's Army Game.* CASOS Technical Report. Available at http://reports-archive.adm.cs.cmu.edu/anon/isri2005/abstracts/05-120.html.

Carlson, Scott. 2011. "Conference Captures College Presidents' Nervousness about the Future of the Liberal Arts." *Chronicle of Higher Education,* January 5. Available at http://www.naicu.edu/news_room/news_detail.asp?id=10388.

Chace, William M. 2009. "The Decline of the English Department." *American Scholar* (Fall). Available at http://www.theamericanscholar.org/the-decline-of-the-english-department.

Charland, Maurice. 1986. "Technological Nationalism." *Canadian Journal of Political and Social Theory* 10 (1): 196–220.

Chartier, Roger. 1989. "Texts, Printings, Readings." In *The New Cultural History,* edited by Lynn Hunt, 154–75. Berkeley: University of California Press.

CHASS. 2006. "CHASS Submission: Productivity Commission Study on Science and Innovation." Available at http://www.chass.org.au/submissions/pdf/SUB20060807TG.pdf.

Chatfield, Tom. 2010. "Do Writers Need Paper?" *Prospect,* October 23. Available at http://www.prospectmagazine.co.uk/2010/10/books-electronic-publishing.

Chomsky, Noam. 1965. *Aspects of the Theory of Syntax.* Cambridge, MA: MIT Press.

"CIA Director Calls for a National Commitment to Language Proficiency at Foreign Language Summit." 2010. Central Intelligence Agency, December 8. Available at https://www.cia.gov/news-information/press-releases-statements/press-release-2010/foreign-language-summit.html.

Cifaldi, Frank, and Jeffrey Fleming. 2007. "We See Farther—a History of Electronic Arts." *Gamasutra,* February 16. Available at http://www.gamasutra.com/view/feature/1711/we_see_farther__a_history_of_.php.

The Coca-Cola Company. 2012. "Leadership Viewpoints: Wendy Clark." Available at http://www.thecoca-colacompany.com/dynamic/leadershipviewpoints/profiles/wendy-clark.html.

Cohen, Nick. 2011. "Academia Plays into the Hands of the Right." *The Guardian*, January 29. Available at http://www.guardian.co.uk/commentisfree/2011/jan/30/nick-cohen-higher-education-cuts.

Cohen, Patricia. 2009. "In Tough Times, the Humanities Must Justify Their Worth." *New York Times*, February 24. Available at http://www.nytimes.com/2009/02/25/books/25human.html.

———. 2010. "Digital Keys for Unlocking the Humanities' Riches." *New York Times*, November 16. Available at http://www.nytimes.com/2010/11/17/arts/17digital.html.

Coleridge, Samuel Taylor. 1839. *On the Constitution of Church and State according to the Idea of Each. II: Lay Sermons.* Edited by Henry Nelson Coleridge. London: William Pickering.

"College Tuition Hike in California Sparks Protests." 2009. PBS NewsHour. Available at http://www.pbs.org/newshour/bb/education/july-dec09/fee hikes_11-20.html.

Commission of the European Communities. 2006. "White Paper on a European Communication Policy." Available at http://europa.eu/documents/comm/white_papers/pdf/com2006_35_en.pdf.

Committee on the National Plan for the Future of the Humanities. 2009. *Sustainable Humanities: Report from the Committee on the National Plan for the Future of the Humanities.* Amsterdam: Commissie National Plan Toekomst Geesteswetenschappen/Amsterdam University Press.

Consalvo, Mia. 2006. "Console Video Games and Global Corporations: Creating a Hybrid Culture." *New Media and Society* 8 (1): 117–37.

Corbett, Charles J., and Richard P. Turco. 2006. *Sustainability in the Motion Picture Industry.* Report prepared for the Integrated Waste Management Board of the State of California. Available at http://personal.anderson.ucla.edu/charles.corbett/papers/mpis_report.pdf.

Cornell University Library. 2005. "Faculty Senate Resolution." May 17. Available at http://www.library.cornell.edu/scholarlycomm/resolution.html.

Costa, Marisa Vorraber, Rosa Hessel Silveira, and Luis Henrique Sommer. 2003. "Estudos culturais, educação e pedagogia." *Revista Brasileira de Educação* 23:36–61.

Council for the Humanities, Arts and Social Sciences. 2005. *Measures of Quality and Impact of Publicly Funded Research in the Humanities, Arts and Social Sciences.* Canberra: Council for Humanities, Arts and Social Sciences.

———. 2012. "About the Council: Overview." Available at http://www.chass.org.au/about.

Cowden, Stephen J. 2005. "Reed Elsevier's Reply." *The Lancet* 366 (September 10): 889–90.

Craig, Kathleen. 2006. "Dead in Iraq: It's No Game." *Wired*, June 6. Available at http://www.wired.com/gaming/gamingreviews/news/2006/06/71052.

Creative Commons. n.d. "Attribution 2.0 Generic (CC BY 2.0)." Available at http://creativecommons.org/licenses/by/2.0. Accessed February 28, 2012.

Crossick, Geoffrey, Nicholas Penny, Rick Trainor, Nicholas Kenyon, Nigel Carrington, Sandy Nairne, Edward Acton, Andrew Burnett, Malcolm Gillies, Colin Riordan, Paul Curran, Colin Jones, Richard Mantle, and Clare Matterson. 2010. "Don't Ditch Arts Funding in Favour of Science. It's Vital to Our Society." *The Observer*, February 28. Available at http://www.guardian.co.uk/theobserver/2010/feb/28/observer-letters-arts-funding.

Cultural Values: Journal for Cultural Research. 2002. Special issue, 6 (1–2).

Cunningham, Stuart. 1992. *Framing Culture: Criticism and Policy in Australia.* Sydney: Allen and Unwin.

———. 2001. "From Cultural to Creative Industries: Theory, Industry, and Policy Implications." In "Convergence, Creative Industries and Civil Society: The New Cultural Policy," edited by Colin Mercer. Special issue, *Culturelink* (Zagreb: Institute for International Relations): 19–32.

———. 2006a. "Business Needs Crash Course in Appreciation." *Australian Financial Review*, August 14, 36.

———. 2006b. "Don't Undervalue Humanities." *Australian Financial Review*, September 18, 42.

———. 2007a. "Oh, the Humanities! Australia's Innovation System out of Kilter." *Australian Universities Review* 49 (1–2): 28–30.

———. 2007b. "Taking Arts into the Digital Era." *Courier Mail*, June 22. Available at http://www.onlineopinion.com.au/view.asp?article=6031.

———. 2009a. "Can Creativity Be Taught? And Should It Be?" *Australian PolicyOnline*, December 7. Available at http://www.apo.org.au/commentary/can-creativity-be-taught-and-should-it-be.

———. 2009b. "Creative Industries as a Globally Contestable Policy Field." *Chinese Journal of Communication* 2 (1): 13–24.

———. 2009c. "Trojan Horse or Rorschach Blot? Creative Industries Discourse around the World." *International Journal of Cultural Policy* 15 (4): 375–86.

———. 2011. "Developments in Measuring the 'Creative' Workforce." *Cultural Trends* 20 (1): 25–40.

Cushman, Mike. 2011. "Crash Was Fuelled by Academic Journals." *The Guardian*, February 18. Available at http://www.guardian.co.uk/education/2011/feb/19/crash-fuelled-by-academic-journals.

Dahlström, Margareta, and Brita Hermelin. 2007. "Creative Industries, Spatiality and Flexibility: The Example of Film Production." *Norsk Geografisk Tiddskrift—Norwegian Journal of Geography* 61 (3): 111–21.

Dames, Nicholas. 2011. "Why Bother?" *n+1*, April 13. Available at http://nplusonemag.com/why-bother.

Danan, Martine. 2009. "Marketing the Hollywood Blockbuster in France." In *The Contemporary Hollywood Reader*, edited by Toby Miller, 376–86. London: Routledge.

Darnton, Robert. 2011. "5 Myths about the 'Information Age.'" *Chronicle Review*, April 17. Available at http://chronicle.com/article/5-Myths-About-the-Information/127105.

Davidson, Cathy N. 2008. "Humanities 2.0: Promise, Perils, Predictions." *PMLA* 123 (3): 707–17.

Davidson, Cathy N., and David Theo Goldberg. 2004. "Engaging the Humanities." *Profession*, 2004, 42–62.

Dean Dad. 2011. "Liberal Arts or General Education?" *Inside Higher Ed*, January 10. Available at http://www.insidehighered.com/blogs/confessions_of _a_community_college_dean/liberal_arts_or_general_education.

Deck, Andy. 2004. "No Quarter: Demilitarizing the Playground." *Art Context*. Available at http://artcontext.org/crit/essays/noQuarter.

Defense Advanced Research Projects Agency (DARPA). n.d. "Opportunities at DARPA: Young Faculty Award." Available at http://www.darpa.mil/ Opportunities/Universities/Young_Faculty.aspx. Accessed March 1, 2012.

———. n.d. "Universities." Available at http://www.darpa.mil/Opportunities/ Universities. Accessed March 1, 2012.

DeLappe, Joseph. 2006. "dead-in-iraq." Available at http://www.unr.edu/art/ delappe/gaming/dead_in_iraq/dead_in_iraq%20jpegs.html.

DeLillo, Don. 1986. *White Noise*. London: Picador.

Department of Defense. 2010. "*UrbanSim*—Counterinsurgency Computer Training Game." *Armed with Science* podcast, March 3. Available at http:// science.dodlive.mil/2010/03/page/3/.

Deresiewicz, William. 2011. "Faulty Towers: The Crisis in Higher Education." *The Nation*, May 4. Available at http://www.thenation.com/article/160410/ faulty-towers-crisis-higher-education.

Desrochers, Donna M., Colleen M. Lenihan, and Jane V. Wellman. 2010. *Trends in College Spending 1998–2008: Where Does the Money Come From? Where Does It Go?* Washington, DC: Delta Cost Project/Lumina Foundation for Education.

Dewatripont, Mathias, Victor Ginsburgh, Patrick Legros, Alexis Walckiers, Jean-Pierre Devroey, Marianne Dujardin, Françoise Vandooren, and Marie-Dominique Heusse. 2006. *Study on the Economic and Technical Evolution of the Scientific Publication Markets in Europe*. Brussels: DG-Research, European Commission.

Donoghue, Frank. 2010. "Can the Humanities Survive the 21st Century?" *Chronicle of Higher Education*, September 5. Available at http://chronicle .com/article/Can-the-Humanities-Survive-the/124222.

Douglas, Mary. 1966. *Purity and Danger: An Analysis of Concepts of Pollution and Taboo*. London: Routledge and Kegan Paul.

Dreher, C. 2002. "What Drives US Cities?" *Hamilton Spectator*, July 20.

Dufresne, Todd. 2010. "To SSHRC or Not to SSHRC?" *Academic Matters*, November 26. Available at http://www.academicmatters.ca/2010/11/to-sshrc-or-not-to-sshrc/.

Dyer-Witheford, Nick, and Greig S. de Peuter. 2006. "'EA Spouse' and the Crisis of Video Game Labour: Enjoyment, Exclusion, Exploitation, and Exodus." *Canadian Journal of Communication* 31 (3): 599–617.

———. 2009. *Games of Empire: Global Capitalism and Video Games.* Minneapolis: University of Minnesota Press.

Dyson, Esther, George Gilder, George Keyworth, and Alvin Toffler. 1994. "Cyberspace and the American Dream: A Magna Carta for the Knowledge Age." Release 1.2. Progress and Freedom Foundation. Available at http://pff.org/issues-pubs/futureinsights/fi1.2magnacarta.html.

Early, Gerald. 2009. "The Humanities and Social Change." *Daedalus* 138 (1): 52–57.

ea_spouse. 2004. "EA: The Human Story." *Live Journal*, November 11. Available at http://ea-spouse.livejournal.com/274.html.

Eco, Umberto. 1972. "Towards a Semiotic Inquiry into the Television Message." Translated by Paolo Splendore. *Working Papers in Cultural Studies* 3:103–21.

———. 1979. *The Role of the Reader.* Bloomington: Indiana University Press.

Edelstein, Dan. 2010. "How Is Innovation Taught? On the Humanities and the Knowledge Economy." *Liberal Education* 96 (1). Available at http://www.aacu.org/liberaleducation/le-wi10/le-wi10_Innovation.cfm.

Edgar, David. 2000. "Playing Shops, Shopping Plays: The Effect of the Internal Market on Television Drama." In *British Television Drama: Critical Perspectives*, edited by Jonathan Bignell, Stephen Lacey, and Madeleine Macmurraugh-Kavanagh, 73–77. Houndmills, UK: Palgrave Macmillan.

Edwards, David. 2010. *The Lab: Creativity and Culture.* Cambridge, MA: Harvard University Press.

Ehrenreich, Ben. 2011. "The Death of the Book." *Los Angeles Review of Books*, April 18. Available at http://lareviewofbooks.org/post/4659371294/the-death-of-the-book.

Eisenhower, Dwight D. 1972. "Liberty Is at Stake." In *SuperState: Readings in the Military-Industrial Complex*, edited by Herbert I. Schiller and Joseph D. Phillips, 29–34. Urbana: University of Illinois Press.

Ekman, Richard. 1995. "The Foundation's Role in Support of the Humanities: 1995 Annual Report." Available at http://www.mellon.org/news_publications/annual-reports-essays/presidents-essays/the-foundation-s-role-in-support-of-the-humanities.

Electronic Publishing Services Ltd. 2006. *UK Scholarly Journals: 2006 Baseline Report: An Evidence-Based Analysis of Data concerning Scholarly Journal Publishing.* London: Research Information Network, Research Councils UK, and Department of Trade and Industry.

Ellis, John. 2005. "Media Studies: Discuss." BBC News, August 18. Available at http://news.bbc.co.uk/2/hi/uk_news/magazine/4158902.stm.

Ellison, Julie. 2009. "This American Life: How Are the Humanities Public?" In *Humanities Indicators Prototype*, American Academy of Arts and Sciences. Available at http://www.humanitiesindicators.org/essays/ellison.pdf.

Else, Gerald F. 1969. "The Old and the New Humanities." *Daedalus* 98 (3): 803–8.

Emerson, Ralph Waldo. 1909. *Essays and English Traits*. New York: P. F. Collier.

Enger, Rolf C., Steven K. Jones, and Dana H. Born. 2010. "Commitment to Liberal Education at the United States Air Force Academy." *Liberal Education* 96 (2). Available at http://www.aacu.org/liberaleducation/le-sp10/LESP10_Commitment.cfm.

"E-Publish or Perish." 2010. *The Economist*, April 3, 65–66.

European Commission. 2009. *Emerging Trends in Socio-economic Sciences and Humanities in Europe: The METRIS Report*. Brussels: European Commission.

Ferguson, Charles. 2010. "Larry Summers and the Subversion of Economics." *Chronicle Review*, October 3. Available at http://chronicle.com/article/Larry-Summersthe/124790.

Fish, Stanley. 2008a. "The Uses of the Humanities, Part Two." *New York Times*, January 13. Available at http://opinionator.blogs.nytimes.com/2008/01/13/the-uses-of-the-humanities-part-two.

———. 2008b. "Will the Humanities Save Us?" *New York Times*, January 6. Available at http://opinionator.blogs.nytimes.com/2008/01/06/will-the-humanities-save-us.

———. 2010. "The Crisis of the Humanities Officially Arrives." *New York Times*, October 11. Available at http://opinionator.blogs.nytimes.com/2010/10/11/the-crisis-of-the-humanities-officially-arrives.

Flammang, Lucretia A. 2007. "The Place of the Humanities at a Military Academy." *Academe* (July–August). Available at http://www.aaup.org/AAUP/pubsres/academe/2007/JA/Feat/flam.htm.

Florida, Richard. 2002. *The Rise of the Creative Class and How It's Transforming Work, Leisure and Everyday Life*. New York: Basic Books.

Folbre, Nancy. 2010. "Ethics for Economists." *New York Times*, November 8. Available at http://economix.blogs.nytimes.com/2010/11/08/ethics-for-economists.

Forbes, Steve. 2011. "Dinosaur U." *Forbes*, February 28. Available at http://www.forbes.com/forbes/2011/0228/opinions-steve-forbes-fact-comment-dinosaur-u.html.

Foucault, Michel. 1986a. "Of Other Spaces." Translated by Jay Miskowiec. *Diacritics* 16 (1): 22–27.

———. 1986b. *The Use of Pleasure: The History of Sexuality*. Vol. 2. Translated by Robert Hurley. London: Penguin Books.

———. 1988. *The Care of the Self: Volume Three of "The History of Sexuality."* Translated by Robert Hurley. New York: Vintage.

———. 2001. *Dits et écrits 1954–1988*. Vol. 2, *1967–1988*. Edited by Daniel Defert and François Ewald, with Jacques Lagrange. Paris: Quarto Gallimard.

Foucault, Michel, and Richard Sennett. 1982. "Sexuality and Solitude." *Humanities in Review* 1:3–21.

Fox, Adam. 2003. "Talking about My Generation." *The Guardian*, May 23. Available at http://www.guardian.co.uk/education/2003/may/23/higher education.comment.

Franke, Richard J. 2009. "The Power of the Humanities and a Challenge to Humanists." *Daedalus* 138 (1): 13–23.

Freeman, Alan. 2007. *London's Creative Sector: 2007 Update*. Working Paper 22. London: Greater London Authority.

Friedberg, Judy. 2011. "Cribsheet 07.02.11." *The Guardian*, February 7. Available at http://www.guardian.co.uk/education/2011/feb/07/cribsheet-education-diet-plan.

Frow, John. 1999. "Cultural Studies and the Neoliberal Imagination." *Yale Journal of Criticism* 12 (2): 424–30.

———. 2005. "The Public Humanities." *Modern Language Review* (Supplement): 269–80.

Fugh-Berman, Adriane J. 2010. "The Haunting of Medical Journals: How Ghostwriting Sold 'HRT.'" *PLoS Medicine* 7 (9): e1000335.

Fulbright, J. William. 1972. "Science and the Universities in the Military-Industrial Complex." In *SuperState: Readings in the Military-Industrial Complex*, edited by Herbert I. Schiller and Joseph D. Phillips, 173–78. Urbana: University of Illinois Press.

García Canclini, Néstor. 1995. *Hybrid Cultures: Strategies for Entering and Leaving Modernity*. Minneapolis: University of Minnesota Press.

———. 2004. *Diferentes, desiguales y desconectados: Mapas de la interculturalidad*. Barcelona: Editorial Gedisa.

Garfinkel, Harold. 1992. *Studies in Ethnomethodology*. Cambridge, UK: Polity Press.

Garne, D., M. Watson, S. Chapman, and F. Byrne. 2005. "Environmental Tobacco Smoke Research Published in the Journal *Indoor and Built Environment* and Associations with the Tobacco Industry." *The Lancet* 365 (9461): 804–9.

Garnham, Nicholas. 2005. "From Cultural to Creative Industries: An Analysis of the Implications of the 'Creative Industries' Approach to Arts and Media Policy Making in the United Kingdom." *International Journal of Cultural Policy* 11 (1): 15–29.

Gates, Robert. 2010. "Lecture at Duke University (All-Volunteer Force)." September 29. Available at http://www.defense.gov/speeches/speech.aspx?speechid=1508.

Geiger, Roger L. 2009. "Taking the Pulse of the Humanities: Higher Education in the Humanities Indicators Project." *Humanities Indicators Prototype*. Available at http://www.humanitiesindicators.org/essays/geiger.pdf.

Gellner, Ernest. 1964. "The Crisis in the Humanities and the Mainstream of Philosophy." In *Crisis in the Humanities*, edited by J. H. Plumb, 45–81. Harmondsworth, UK: Penguin.

Gibson, Chris, and Natascha Klocker. 2004. "Academic Publishing as 'Creative' Industry, and Recent Discourses of 'Creative Economies': Some Critical Reflections." *Area* 36 (4): 423–34.

Gillies, Malcolm. 2006. "Preface." In *Collaborating across the Sectors: The Relationship between the Humanities, Arts and Social Sciences (HASS) and Science, Technology, Engineering and Medicine (STEM) Sectors*, by Jenni Metcalfe, Michelle Riedlinger, Anne Pisarski, and John Gardner, 3. Council for the Humanities, Arts and Social Sciences Occasional Paper 3. Canberra, Australia: CHASS.

———. 2009. "The Priced and the Priceless: Humanities and Philanthropy in Dark Times." *Australian Book Review*, no. 312 (June): 34–39.

———. 2010. "The Humanities: Location, Discipline, Value." Paper presented at Valuing the Humanities Conference, Research Centre for Human Values, Chinese University of Hong Kong, October 14.

Giroux, Henry A. 2007. *The University in Chains: Confronting the Military-Industrial-Academic Complex*. Boulder, CO: Paradigm Publishers.

———. 2008. "Against the Militarized Academy." *Truthout*, November 20. Available at http://archive.truthout.org/112008J.

Giroux, Henry A., and Kostas Myrsiades, eds. 2001. *Beyond the Corporate University*. Lanham, MD: Rowman and Littlefield.

Givler, Peter. 2002. "University Press Publishing in the United States." In *Scholarly Publishing: Books, Journals, Publishers and Libraries in the Twentieth Century*, edited by Richard E. Abel and Lyman W. Newlin, 107–20. New York: Wiley.

Global Alliance for Cultural Diversity. 2002. *Understanding Creative Industries: Cultural Statistics for Public Policy-Making*. Paris: UNESCO.

Goldberg, David Theo. 2011. "The AfterLife of the Humanities: PostHumanities, Poor Theory, and Public Reason." Manuscript in possession of the author.

Goodman, David. 2009. "A Few Good Kids?" *Mother Jones*, September–October. Available at http://motherjones.com/politics/2009/09/few-good-kids.

Gorz, André. 2004. "Économie de la connaissance, exploitation des savoirs: Entretien réalisé par Yann Moulier Boutang et Carlo Vercellone." *Multitudes*. Available at http://multitudes.samizdat.net/Economie-de-la-connaissance.

Gould, Thomas H. P. 2009. "The Future of Academic Publishing: Application of the Long-Tail Theory." *Publishing Research Quarterly* 25 (4): 232–45.

Grafton, Anthony. 2010. "Scholars of the World Unite!" *National Interest*, December 16. Available at http://nationalinterest.org/bookreview/scholars-the-world-unite-4578.

———. 2011. "History under Attack." *Perspectives* (January). Available at http://www.historians.org/Perspectives/issues/2011/1101/1101pre1.cfm.

Greco, Albert N., and Robert M. Wharton. 2010. "The Market Demand for University Press Books 2008–15." *Journal of Scholarly Publishing* 42 (1): 1–15.

Greenblatt, Stephen. 2002. "A Special Letter from Stephen Greenblatt," May 28. Available at http://www.mla.org/scholarly_pub.

Gundur, N. S. 2010. "Academics in the Armed Forces: A Critical Evaluation of English Language Curricula at the National Defence Academy (India)." *Journal of Language Teaching and Research* 1 (4): 401–5.

Hall, Stuart. 2004. "Graham Martin: Literary Critic and Cultural Studies Innovator." *The Guardian*, February 12. Available at http://www.guardian.co.uk/news/2004/feb/12/guardianobituaries.obituaries.

Harmon, Amy. 2003. "More Than Just a Game, but How Close to Reality?" *New York Times*, April 3. Available at http://www.nytimes.com/2003/04/03/technology/more-than-just-a-game-but-how-close-to-reality.html.

Harney, Stefano. 2002. *State Work: Public Administration and Mass Intellectuality*. Durham, NC: Duke University Press.

———. 2010. "The Heart of Good Business." *Times Higher Education*, November 18. Available at http://www.timeshighereducation.co.uk/story.asp?storyCode=414296&sectioncode=26.

Hart Research Associates. 2010. *Raising the Bar: Employers' Views on College Learning in the Wake of the Economic Downturn*. Washington, DC: Hart Research Associates.

Healy, Michael. 2008. "Experimentation and Innovation in U.S. Publishing Today: Findings from the Book Industry Study Group." *Publishing Research Quarterly* 24 (4): 233–39.

Hebert, James. 2005. "Band of Brothers." *San Diego Union-Tribune*, November 6. Available at http://legacy.signonsandiego.com/uniontrib/20051106/news_lz1a06ictech.html.

Heitman, Danny. 2011. "How Can Obama Save Our Economy and Our Democracy? Humanities Education." *Christian Science Monitor*, February 18. Available at http://www.csmonitor.com/Commentary/Opinion/2011/0218/How-can-Obama-save-our-economy-and-our-democracy-Humanities-education.

Hennigan, W. J. 2010. "Computer Simulation Is a Growing Reality for Instruction." *Los Angeles Times*, November 2. Available at http://articles.latimes.com/2010/nov/02/business/la-fi-virtual-reality-20101102.

Henwood, Doug. 2010. "I'm Borrowing My Way through College." *Left Business Observer* 125 (February). Available at http://leftbusinessobserver.com/College.html.

Hesmondhalgh, David. 2008. "Cultural and Creative Industries." In *The SAGE Handbook of Cultural Analysis*, edited by Tony Bennett and John Frow, 552–69. Los Angeles: Sage.

Higgins, Charlotte. 2010. "Antony Beevor: Journalism Has Spoilt the Ground for Historians." *The Guardian*, May 31. Available at http://www.guardian.co.uk/uk/2010/may/31/antony-beevor-iraq-hay-festival.

Hilmes, Michele. 2005. "The Bad Object: Television in the American Academy." *Cinema Journal* 45 (1): 111–17.

Hodges, Lucy. 2009. "Popular Culture: Why Chinese Students Are Getting Creative." *The Independent*, January 8. Available at http://www.independent

.co.uk/news/education/higher/popular-culture-why-chinese-students-are-getting-creative-1231005.html.

Hogan, Phil. 2004. "Television Studies." *The Observer*, February 1. Available at http://www.guardian.co.uk/lifeandstyle/2004/feb/01/features.familyand relationships.

Hoggart, Richard. 1957. *The Uses of Literacy: Aspects of Working Class Life.* London: Chatto and Windus.

———. 1973. *Speaking to Each Other.* Vol. 1, *About Society.* Harmondsworth, UK: Penguin.

———. 2005. *Mass Media in a Mass Society: Myth and Reality.* London: Continuum.

Hohendahl, Peter Uwe. 2005. "The Future of the Research University and the Fate of the Humanities." *Cultural Critique* 61:1–21.

Hough, Graham. 1964. "Crisis in Literary Education." In *Crisis in the Humanities*, edited by J. H. Plumb, 96–109. Harmondsworth, UK: Penguin.

Huijgh, Ellen. 2007. "Diversity United? Towards a European Cultural Industries Policy." *Policy Studies* 28 (3): 209–24.

Humphreys, Debra. 2009. *Making the Case for Liberal Education: Responding to Challenges.* Washington, DC: Association of American Colleges and Universities.

———. 2010. "*Wired* Names the Neoliberal Arts—and They Look a Lot Like AAC&U's Essential Learning Outcomes." Association of American Colleges and Universities, October 29. Available at http://blog.aacu.org/index.php/2010/10/29/wired-names-the-neoliberal-arts.

Hunter, Ian. 1988a. "Providence and Profit: Speculations in the Genre Market." *Southern Review* 22 (3): 211–23.

———. 1988b. "Setting Limits to Culture." *New Formations* 4 (1): 103–23.

———. 1996. "Is English an Emancipatory Discipline?" *Australian Humanities Review.* Available at http://www.australianhumanitiesreview.org/archive/Issue-April-1996/Hunter.html.

———. 2006. "The History of Theory." *Critical Inquiry* 33 (1): 78–112.

———. 2008. "Critical Response II: Talking about My Generation." *Critical Inquiry* 34 (3): 583–600.

Iannone, Carol. 2008. "Liberal Education at the Academy: A Conversation with West Point Professor David Bedey." *Academic Questions* 21 (1): 79–97.

Ianziti, Gary. 2007. "Traditional Humanities Out: Creative Industries In." *On Line Opinion*, May 10. Available at http://www.onlineopinion.com.au/view.asp?article=5832.

IGN Entertainment. 2011. "We're IGN Entertainment, an Online Media and Services Company Obsessed with Gaming, Entertainment and Everything Guys Enjoy." Available at http://corp.ign.com/about.

"Inappropriate Behaviour on *Big Brother* and *Little Britain* Are Leading to Classrooms of Vicky Pollards, Says ATL." 2009. ATL, March 30. Available at http://www.atl.org.uk/media-office/media-archive/Inappropriate-behaviour.asp.

Independent Review of Higher Education Funding and Student Finance. 2010. *Securing a Sustainable Future for Higher Education.* Available at http://www.bis.gov.uk/assets/biscore/corporate/docs/s/10-1208-securing-sustainable-higher-education-browne-report.

Institute for Creative Technologies. 2011. "USC Institute for Creative Technologies Receives $135 Million Contract Extension from U.S. Army." September 1. Available at http://ict.usc.edu/news/item/usc_institute_for_creative_technologies_receives_135_million_contract_exten.

———. 2012. "Sergeant Star." Available at http://ict.usc.edu/projects/sergeant_star/C40.

International Association of Scientific, Technical, and Medical Publishers. 2007. "Brussels Declaration on STM [Scientific, Technical and Medical] Publishing." Available at http://www.stm-assoc.org/brussels-declaration/.

International Organization for Migration. n.d. "Facts and Figures." Available at http://www.iom.int/jahia/Jahia/about-migration/facts-and-figures/lang/en. Accessed March 1, 2012.

International Physicians for the Prevention of Nuclear War, Scientists for Global Responsibility, Campaign against Arms Trade, Europeans for Medical Progress, and Physicians for Social Responsibility. 2005. "Reed Elsevier and the International Arms Trade." *The Lancet* 366:889.

Jacobson, Howard. 2010. "You'll Never Catch Me Going on a March." *The Independent*, December 11. Available at http://www.independent.co.uk/opinion/commentators/howard-jacobson/howard-jacobson-youll-never-catch-me-going-on-a-march-2157452.html.

Jaschik, Scott. 2011. "Rejecting Double Blind." *Times Higher Education*, May 31. Available at http://www.timeshighereducation.co.uk/story.asp?sectioncode=26&storycode=416353&c=1.

Jodhpur Initiatives. 2005. *Asia-Pacific Creative Communities: A Strategy for the 21st Century.* Bangkok: UNESCO.

Jorgenson, Andrew K., Brett Clark, and Jeffrey Kentor. 2010. "Militarization and the Environment: A Panel Study of Carbon Dioxide Emissions and the Ecological Footprints of Nations, 1970–2000." *Global Environmental Politics* 10 (1): 7–29.

Kant, Immanuel. 1952. *The Critique of Judgement.* Translated by James Creed Meredith. New York: Oxford University Press.

———. 1991. *Political Writings.* 2nd ed. Edited by H. Reiss. Translated by H. B. Nisbet. Cambridge: Cambridge University Press.

Kaufman-Wills Group, LLC. 2005. *The Facts about Open Access: A Study of the Financial and Non-financial Effects of Alternative Business Models for Scholarly Journals.* Worthing, UK: Association of Learned and Professional Society Publishers, American Association for the Advancement of Science, High Wire Press/Stanford Libraries, Association of American Medical Colleges.

Keane, Michael. 2006. "From Made in China to Created in China." *International Journal of Cultural Studies* 9 (3): 285–96.

Keith, Bruce. 2010. "The Transformation of West Point as a Liberal Arts College." *Liberal Education* 96 (2). Available at http://www.aacu.org/liberal education/le-sp10/LESP10_Keith.cfm.

Kermode, Frank. 1997. "The Academy vs. the Humanities." *Atlantic Monthly*, August, 93–96. Available at http://www.theatlantic.com/past/docs/issues/ 97aug/academy.htm.

Kerr, Clark. 1963. *The Uses of the University*. Cambridge, MA: Harvard University Press.

Kiley, Kevin. 2011. "Decline of 'Western Civ'?" *Inside Higher Ed*, May 19. Available at http://www.insidehighered.com/news/2011/05/19/national_association_ of_scholars_report_finds_no_mandatory_western_civilization_courses _at_top_universities.

Kittler, Friedrich. 2004. "Universities: Wet, Hard, Soft, and Harder." *Critical Inquiry* 31 (1): 244–55.

Kittross, John Michael. 1999. "A History of the BEA." *Feedback* 40 (2). Available at http://www.beaweb.org/pdfs/beahistory.pdf.

Kotkin, Joel. 2001. *The New Geography: How the Digital Revolution Is Reshaping the American Landscape*. New York: Random House.

Kull, Steve, Clay Ramsay, Evan Lewis, and Stefan Subias. 2011. *Competing Budget Priorities: The Public, the House, and the White House*. Baltimore: Program for Public Consultation and Knowledge Networks.

Kultur Macht Europa. 2007, June 7. "Culture Powers Europe." Available at http://www.kultur-macht-europa.de/47.html?&no_cache=1&L=1&tx _ttnews[tt_news]=138&cHash=d8fe0dfdce.

Kundnani, Arun. 2004. "Wired for War: Military Technology and the Politics of Fear." *Race and Class* 46 (1): 116–25.

Kyrillidou, Martha, and Mark Young. 2006. *ARL Statistics 2004–05*. Washington, DC: Association of Research Libraries.

The *Lancet* and the *Lancet*'s International Advisory Board. 2005. "Reed Elsevier and the Arms Trade." *The Lancet* 366 (September): 868.

Lanchester, John. 2007. "It's a Steal." *The Guardian*, April 7. Available at http://www.guardian.co.uk/books/2007/apr/07/featuresreviews.guardian review2.

Lasch, Christopher. 1979. *The Culture of Narcissism: American Life in an Age of Diminishing Expectations*. New York: Warner Books.

Latour, Bruno. 1993. *We Have Never Been Modern*. Translated by Catherine Porter. Cambridge, MA: Harvard University Press.

Lawrence, D. H. 1961. *Lady Chatterley's Lover*. Harmondsworth, UK: Penguin.

Lea, Richard. 2010. "Books Overtake Games as Most Numerous iPhone Apps." *The Guardian*, March 9. Available at http://www.guardian.co.uk/ books/2010/mar/09/books-overtake-games-iphone-apps.

Leach, Jim. 2011. "The Humanities and National Security." Briefing on the Humanities in the 21st Century, United States Capitol, Washington, DC, May 19.

Leaning, Jennifer. 2000. "Environment and Health: 5. Impact of War." *Canadian Medical Association Journal* 163 (9): 1157–61.

Leavis, F. R. 1947. "The Literary Discipline and Liberal Education." *Sewanee Review* 55 (4): 586–609.

———. 1956. "Literary Studies: A Reply." *Universities Quarterly* 11 (1): 14–27.

———. 1972. *Nor Shall My Sword: Discourses on Pluralism, Compassion and Social Hope.* New York: Barnes and Noble.

Lenoir, Timothy. 2003. "Programming Theaters of War: Gamemakers as Soldiers." In *Bombs and Bandwidth: The Emerging Relationship between Information Technology and Security*, edited by Robert Latham, 175–98. New York: New Press.

Levering, Robert, Milton Moskowitz, Ann Harrington, and Christopher Tzacyk. 2003. "100 Best Companies to Work For." *Fortune*, January 20, 127–52.

Levine, George, Peter Brooks, Jonathan Culler, Marjorie Garber, E. Ann Kaplan, and Catharine R. Stimpson. 1989. *Speaking for the Humanities.* Occasional Paper 7. New York: American Council of Learned Societies.

LeVine, Mark. 2011. "Mid East Battle of the Sociologists." *Al Jazeera*, May 11. Available at http://english.aljazeera.net/indepth/opinion/2011/03/2011 31011111755251.html.

Lewis, Justin. 1983. *Cable and Community Programming.* London: Greater London Council.

———. 1985. *The Audience for Community Radio.* London: Greater London Council.

———, ed. 1986. *A Sporting Chance—a Review of the GLC Recreation Policy.* London: Greater London Council.

———. 1991. *Art, Culture, and Enterprise: The Politics of Art and the Cultural Industries.* London: Routledge.

Lewis, Justin, Sanna Inthorn, and Karin Wahl-Jorgensen. 2005. *Citizens or Consumers? What the Media Tell Us about Political Participation.* Maidenhead, UK: Open University Press.

Lightfoot, Liz. 2005. "Students Mark Down Media and Tourism Degrees." *The Telegraph*, September 8. Available at http://www.telegraph.co.uk/news/uknews/1497885/Students-mark-down-media-and-tourism-degrees.html.

Linklater, Magnus. 2006. "I Don't Want to Spoil the Party. . . ." *The Times*, November 8. Available at http://www.timesonline.co.uk/tol/comment/columnists/magnus_linklater/article629022.ece.

"The List of Industry Stars." 2007. *Fortune*, March 5. Available at http://money.cnn.com/magazines/fortune/fortune_archive/2007/03/19/8402372/index.htm.

Long, Sheri Spaine. 2010. "Will Peer Review Still Function and How?" *Journal of Scholarly Publishing* 42 (1): 67–70.

Lovink, Geert, and Ned Rossiter, eds. 2007. *MyCreativity Reader: A Critique of Creative Industries.* Amsterdam: Institute of Network Cultures.

Lowry, Howard F. 1941. "The Old and the New Humanities." *Classical Journal* 36 (4): 197–210.

Lyotard, Jean-François. 1988. *La condition postmoderne: Rapport sur le savoir.* Paris: Les Éditions de Minuit.

Macedonia, Mike. 2002. "Games, Simulation, and the Military Education Dilemma." In *The Internet and the University: 2001 Forum*, 157–67. Boulder, CO: Educause.

Macherey, Pierre. 1977. "Culture and Politics: Interview with Pierre Macherey." Edited and translated by Colin Mercer and Jean Radford. *Red Letters* 5:3–9.

———. 2007. "The Literary Thing." Translated by Audrey Wasser. *Diacritics* 37 (4): 21–30.

Machlup, Fritz. 1958. "Can There Be Too Much Research?" *Science* 128 (335): 1320–25.

———. 1962. *The Production and Distribution of Knowledge in the United States.* Princeton, NJ: Princeton University Press.

Manifesto for Higher Education. 2011. Available at http://hemanifesto.tumblr.com/manifesto.

Maniquis, Robert M. 1983. "Marxists and the University: Introduction." *Humanities in Society* 6 (2–3): 133–37.

Mansfield, Alan. 1990. "Cultural Policy Theory and Practice: A New Constellation." *Continuum* 4 (1): 204–14.

Marcus, Carmen. 2005. *Future of Creative Industries: Implications for Research Policy.* Brussels: European Commission Foresight Working Documents Series.

Marcus, George. 1995. "Ethnography in/of the World System: The Emergence of Multi-sited Ethnography." *Annual Review of Anthropology* 24:95–117.

Marcuse, Herbert. 1941. "Some Social Implications of Modern Technology." *Studies in Philosophy and Social Sciences* 9 (3): 414–39.

Martin, Randy. 1998. "Introduction: Education as National Pedagogy." In *Chalk Lines: The Politics of Work in the Managed University*, edited by Randy Martin, 1–29. Durham, NC: Duke University Press.

———. 2009. "Academic Activism." *PMLA* 124 (3): 838–46.

———. 2011. "Taking an Administrative Turn: Derivative Logics for a Recharged Humanities." *Representations* 116 (1): 156–76.

Mattelart, Armand. 2002. "An Archaeology of the Global Era: Constructing a Belief." Translated by Susan Taponier, with Philip Schlesinger. *Media Culture and Society* 24 (5): 591–612.

Mattson, Kevin. 2011. "Cult Stud Mugged: Why We Should Stop Worrying and Learn to Love a Hip English Professor." *Dissent*, January 31. Available at http://dissentmagazine.org/online.php?id=440.

Maxwell, Richard. 2000. "Cultural Studies." In *Understanding Contemporary Society: Theorising the Present*, edited by Gary Browning, Abigail Halcli, and Frank Webster, 281–95. London: Sage.

———. 2002. "Citizens, You Are What You Buy." *Times Higher Education*, December 20. Available at http://www.timeshighereducation.co.uk/story.asp?storyCode=173709&sectioncode=26.

Maxwell, Richard, and Toby Miller. 2012. *Greening the Media*. New York: Oxford University Press.

McChesney, Robert W. 2007. *Communication Revolution: Critical Junctures and the Future of Media*. New York: New Press.

———. 2009. "My Media Studies: Thoughts from Robert W. McChesney." *Television and New Media* 10 (1): 108–9.

McChesney, Robert W., and Dan Schiller. 2002. *The Political Economy of International Communications: Foundations for the Emerging Global Debate over Media Ownership and Regulation*. Geneva: United Nations Research Institute for Social Development.

McCloskey, Deirdre N. 2010. "Disciplines of the World, Unite." *Times Higher Education*, October 7. Available at http://www.timeshighereducation .co.uk/story.asp?storycode=413728.

McCrum, Robert. 2011. "The Web Allows Stories to Be Spun in New Ways." *The Guardian*, May 8. Available at http://www.guardian.co.uk/books/2011/ may/08/deep-media-fiction-web-mccrum.

McDougall, Julian, and Cary Bazalgette. 2011. "Media Studies and Drama Are Not 'Soft.'" *The Guardian*, February 7. Available at http://www.guardian .co.uk/education/2011/feb/08/media-studies-and-drama-not-soft.

McGuigan, Jim. 2004. *Rethinking Cultural Policy*. Maidenhead, UK: Open University Press.

McHoul, Alec, and Tom O'Regan. 1992. "Towards a Paralogics of Textual Technologies: Batman, Glasnost and Relativism in Cultural Studies." *Southern Review* 25 (1): 5–26.

McHoul, Alec, and Mark Rapley. 2001. "Ghost: Do Not Forget; This Visitation / Is but to Whet Thy Almost Blunted Purpose: Culture, Psychology and 'Being Human.'" *Culture and Psychology* 7 (4): 433–51.

McRobbie, Angela. 1996. "All the World's a Stage, Screen or Magazine: When Culture Is the Logic of Late Capitalism." *Media, Culture and Society* 18 (2): 335–42.

Metcalfe, Jenni, Michelle Riedlinger, Anne Pisarski, and John Gardner. 2006. *Collaborating across the Sectors: The Relationship between the Humanities, Arts and Social Sciences (HASS) and Science, Technology, Engineering and Medicine (STEM) Sectors*. Council for the Humanities, Arts and Social Sciences Occasional Paper 3. Canberra, Australia: CHASS.

Miliband, Ralph. 1962. "C. Wright Mills." *New Left Review* 15:15–20.

Miller, Toby. 1993. *The Well-Tempered Self: Citizenship, Culture, and the Postmodern Subject*. Baltimore: Johns Hopkins University Press.

———. 1998. *Technologies of Truth: Cultural Citizenship and the Popular Media*. Minneapolis: University of Minnesota Press.

———. 2001. *SportSex*. Philadelphia: Temple University Press.

———. 2003. "Governmentality or Commodification? US Higher Education." *Cultural Studies* 17 (6): 897–904.

———. 2006. "Sportsex." In *Human Game: Winners and Losers*, edited by Francesca Bonami, Maria Luisa Frisa, and Stefano Tonchi, 338–43. Milan: Edizioni Charta/Fondazione Pitti Discovery.

———. 2007a. "Courageous Competitors." *Press-Enterprise*, March 18, D05.

———. 2007b. *Cultural Citizenship: Cosmopolitanism, Consumerism, and Television in a Neoliberal Age*. Philadelphia: Temple University Press.

———. 2007c. "The Governmentalization and Corporatization of Research." In *Defining Values for Research and Technology: The University's Changing Role*, edited by William T. Greenough, Philip J. McConnaughay, and Jay P. Kesan, 189–209. Lanham, MD: Rowman and Littlefield.

———. 2007d. "Sports and Sex, Forever Intertwined." *Outsports*, March 5. Available at http://outsports.com/columns/20070305tobymiller.htm.

———. 2008a. *Makeover Nation: The United States of Reinvention*. Cleveland: Ohio State University Press.

———. 2008b. "The Pentagon, the University, and the Video Game." *Campus Review*, April 21. Available at http://www.tobymiller.org/images/press/print/campus%20review/thepentagon.pdf.

———. 2009a. "Can Natural Luddites Make Things Explode or Travel Faster? The New Humanities, Cultural Policy Studies, and Creative Industries." In *Media Industries: History, Theory, and Method*, edited by Jennifer Holt and Alisa Perren, 184–98. Malden, UK: Wiley-Blackwell.

———. 2009b. "From Creative to Cultural Industries: Not All Industries Are Cultural, and No Industries Are Creative." *Cultural Studies* 23 (1): 88–99.

———. 2009c. "Governmentality and Commodification: The Keys to Yanqui Academic Hierarchy." In *Towards a Global Autonomous University*, edited by the Edu-Factory Collective, 72–79. New York: Autonomedia.

———. 2010a. "How the Media Biopoliticized Neoliberalism; or, Foucault Meets Marx." *Revista do programa de pós-graduaçao e semiótica* 20:22–31.

———. 2010b. "Journalism and the Question of Citizenship." In *The Routledge Companion to News and Journalism*, edited by Stuart Allan, 397–406. London: Routledge.

Mills, Mark, and Julio Ottino. 2009. "We Need More Renaissance Scientists." *Forbes*, June 3. Available at http://www.forbes.com/2009/06/03/phd-engineering-science-clayton-christensen-mark-mills-innovation-research.html.

"Ministra española dice que la cultura es pilar para el desarollo." 2004. *El universal*, June 30. Available at http://www.eluniverso.com/2004/06/30/0001/1064/7A58C94781354815AE5B05CF7FEB365A.html.

Minogue, Kenneth. 1994. "Philosophy." *Times Literary Supplement*, November 25, 27–28.

Mirrlees, Tanner. 2009. "Digital Militainment by Design: Producing and Playing *SOCOM: U.S. Navy SEALs*." *International Journal of Media and Cultural Politics* 5 (3): 161–81.

MIT Media Lab. n.d. "Sponsorship." Available at http://www.media.mit.edu/sponsorship. Accessed February 27, 2012.

Mitchell, William J., Alan S. Inouye, and Marjory S. Blumenthal, eds. 2003. *Beyond Productivity: Information Technology, Innovation, and Creativity.* Washington, DC: Committee on Information Technology and Creativity, Computer Science and Telecommunications Board, Division on Engineering and Physical Sciences, National Research Council of the National Academies.

Moffatt, Barton, and Carl Elliott. 2007. "Ghost Marketing: Pharmaceutical Companies and Ghostwritten Journal Articles." *Perspectives in Biology and Medicine* 50 (1): 18–31.

Molyneux, John. 2010. "The Politics of Culture." *Socialist Worker,* no. 323. Available at http://johnmolyneux.blogspot.com/2011/01/politics-of-culture .html.

Morgan, John. 2011. "Humanities at Risk in Britain." *Inside Higher Ed,* April 22. Available at http://www.insidehighered.com/news/2011/04/22/are _britain_s_newer_universities_gutting_the_humanities.

Morley, David. 2007. *Media, Modernity and Technology: The Geography of the New.* London: Routledge.

Morris, Chris. 2011. "Electronic Arts Goes 'on the Offensive.'" CNBC, March 2. Available at http://www.cnbc.com/id/41875080.

Morris, Meaghan. 2005. "Humanities for Taxpayers: Some Problems." *New Literary History* 36 (1): 111–29.

———. 2008. "Teaching versus Research? Cultural Studies and the New Class Politics in Knowledge." *Inter-Asia Cultural Studies* 9 (3): 433–50.

Morrison, Nick. 2008. "Mediaocre?" *Times Educational Supplement,* August 15, 8.

Mosco, Vincent. 2004. *The Digital Sublime: Myth, Power, and Cyberspace.* Cambridge, MA: MIT Press.

Muecke, Stephen. 2009. "Cultural Science? The Ecological Critique of Modernity and the Conceptual Habitat of the Humanities." *Cultural Studies* 23 (3): 404–16.

Nader, Laura. 1972. "Up the Anthropologist—Perspectives Gained from Studying Up." In *Reinventing Anthropology,* edited by Dell H. Hymes, 284–311. New York: Pantheon Books.

Nathan, Max. 2007. "The Wrong Stuff? Creative Class Theory and Economic Performance in UK Cities." *Canadian Journal of Regional Science* 3 (Fall): 433–50. Available at http://cjrs-rcsr.org/archives/30-3/NATHAN.pdf.

National Endowment for the Arts. n.d. "Grants: Apply for a Grant." Available at http://arts.gov/grants/apply/AIM/index.html. Accessed March 1, 2012.

National Endowment for the Humanities. 2010. "Humanities Initiatives at Institutions with High Hispanic Enrollment." Available at http://www .neh.gov/grants/guidelines/HI_IHHE.html.

National Foundation on the Arts and the Humanities Act of 1965 (Pub. L. No. 89-209). 1965. Available at http://www.nea.gov/about/Legislation/ Legislation.html.

National Humanities Alliance. 2010. "The Crisis in Humanities Employment for Recent Doctoral Degree Recipients." Available at http://www.nhal liance.org/bm~doc/nha_dp_humempcrisis.pdf.

Naylor, David, and Stephen Toope. 2010. "Don't Swallow These Innovation Nostrums." *Globe and Mail*, August 31. Available at http://www.theglobe andmail.com/news/opinions/dont-swallow-these-innovation-nostrums/ article1688275.

Negri, Antonio. 2007. *goodbye mister socialism*. Paris: Seuil.

New Media Consortium. 2005. "A Global Imperative: The Report of the 21st Century Literacy Summit." Available at http://www.nmc.org/pdf/Global _Imperative.pdf.

Newcomb, Horace. 1996. "Other People's Fictions: Cultural Appropriation, Cultural Integrity, and International Media Strategies." In *Mass Media and Free Trade: NAFTA and the Cultural Industries*, edited by Emile G. McAnany and Kenton T. Wilkinson, 92–109. Austin: University of Texas Press.

Newfield, Christopher. 2003. "The Value of Nonscience." *Critical Inquiry* 29 (3): 508–25.

———. 2004. "Jurassic U: The State of University-Industry Relations." *Social Text* 79:37–66.

———. 2008. "Public Universities at Risk: 7 Damaging Myths." *Chronicle of Higher Education*, October 31, A128.

———. 2009. "Ending the Budget Wars: Funding the Humanities during a Crisis in Higher Education." *Profession*, 2009, 270–84.

———. 2010a. "Avoiding the Coming Higher Ed Wars." *Academe Online*, May–June. Available at http://www.aaup.org/AAUP/pubsres/academe/2010/MJ/ feat/newf.htm.

———. 2010b. "The Structure and Silence of the Cognitariat." *Eurozine*, February 5. Available at http://www.eurozine.com/articles/2010-02-05-newfield-en.html.

Newfield, Christopher, and Gerald Barnett. 2010. "The Federal Stimulus Should Support Research at Public Universities." *Chronicle of Higher Education*, January 3. Available at http://chronicle.com/article/The-Federal-Stimulus-Should/63354.

Newsome, Bruce, and Matthew B. Lewis. 2011. "Rewarding the Cowboy, Punishing the Sniper: The Training Efficacy of Computer-Based Urban Combat Training Environments." *Defence Studies* 11 (1): 120–44.

Nieborg, David B. 2004. "America's Army: More Than a Game." In *Transforming Knowledge into Action through Gaming and Simulation*, edited by Thomas Eberle and Willy Christian Kriz. CD-ROM. Munich: SAGSAGA.

Nussbaum, Martha C. 2009. "91st Commencement Address: 'Not for Profit: Liberal Education and Democratic Citizenship.'" *Commencement Addresses* 18. Available at http://digitalcommons.conncoll.edu/commence/18/.

———. 2010a. "The Liberal Arts Are Not Elitist." *Chronicle of Higher Education*, February 28. Available at http://chronicle.com/article/The-Liberal-Arts-Are-Not/64355.

———. 2010b. *Not for Profit: Why Democracy Needs the Humanities*. Princeton, NJ: Princeton University Press.

Nyquist, Jody, and Donald H. Wulff. 2000. "Recommendations from National Studies on Doctoral Education." Re-envisioning the Ph.D. Available at http://depts.washington.edu/envision/project_resources/national_recommend.html.

Oakley, Francis. 2009. "The Humanities in Liberal Arts Colleges: Another Instance of Collegiate Exceptionalism?" *Daedalus* 138 (1): 35–51.

Oakley, Kate. 2004. "Not So Cool Britannia: The Role of the Creative Industries in Economic Development." *International Journal of Cultural Studies* 7 (1): 67–77.

———. 2006. "Include Us Out—Economic Development and Social Policy in the Creative Industries." *Cultural Trends* 15 (4): 255–73.

———. Forthcoming. "Getting a Foot in the Door: Community Arts and the Workplace." *Vocations and Learning*.

O'Donnell, James J. 2010. "How Scholarly Societies and Scholarly Disciplines Will Change Their Forms of Publication." *Journal of Scholarly Publishing* 42 (1): 46–55.

Organisation for Economic Co-operation and Development. 2004. *Science, Technology and Innovation for the 21st Century. Meeting of the OECD Committee for Scientific and Technological Policy at Ministerial Level, 29–30 January 2004—Final Communique*. Paris: Organisation for Economic Co-operation and Development.

Orwant, John. 2010. "Our Commitment to the Digital Humanities." *Google Blog*, July 14. Available at http://googleblog.blogspot.com/2010/07/our-commitment-to-digital-humanities.html.

Ostriker, Jeremiah P., and Charlotte V. Kuh, assisted by James A. Voytuk. 2003. *Assessing Research-Doctorate Programs: A Methodology Study*. Committee to Examine the Methodology for the Assessment of Research-Doctorate Programs. Washington, DC: National Academies Press.

Parekh, Bhikhu. 2000. *Rethinking Multiculturalism: Cultural Diversity and Political Theory*. Basingstoke, UK: Palgrave.

Parker, Jan. 2008. "Beyond Disciplinarity: Humanities and Supercomplexity." *London Review of Education* 6 (3): 255–66.

Passel, Jeffrey, Wendy Wang, and Paul Taylor. 2010. "Marrying Out: One-in-Seven New U.S. Marriages Is Interracial or Interethnic." Pew Research Center. Available at http://www.pewsocialtrends.org/2010/06/04/marrying-out/.

Paton, Graeme. 2007a. "Media Studies Wastes Good Brains, Says Sugar." *The Telegraph*, May 7. Available at http://www.telegraph.co.uk/news/uknews/1550580/Media-studies-wastes-good-brains-says-Sugar.html.

———. 2007b. "'Soft' A-Levels May Be Harming the Economy." *The Telegraph*, August 15. Available at http://www.telegraph.co.uk/news/uknews/1560326/Soft-A-levels-may-be-harming-the-economy.html.

———. 2008. "Media Studies Degrees 'Require Less Work.'" *The Telegraph*, November 25. Available at http://www.telegraph.co.uk/education/educationnews/3512654/Media-studies-degrees-require-less-work.html.

Pears, Iain. 2010. "Why the Humanities Remain Highly Relevant." *The Guardian*, November 29. Available at http://www.guardian.co.uk/commentisfree/2010/nov/29/funding-cuts-rebalance-education-humanities.

Peck, Jamie. 2007. "The Creativity Fix." *Fronesis* 24. Available at http://www.eurozine.com/articles/2007-06-28-peck-en.html.

Peichi, Chung. 2008. "New Media for Social Change: Globalisation and the Online Gaming Industries of South Korea and Singapore." *Science Technology and Society* 13 (2): 303–23.

Petraeus, David H. 2007. "Beyond the Cloister." *American Interest* 2 (6). Available at http://www.the-american-interest.com/article.cfm?piece=290.

Plumb, J. H. 1964. "Introduction." In *Crisis in the Humanities*, edited by J. H. Plumb, 7–10. Harmondsworth, UK: Penguin.

Poovey, Mary. 2001. "The Twenty-First Century University and the Market: What Price Economic Viability?" *Differences* 12 (1): 1–17.

Porter, Roy. 1991. "History of the Body." In *New Perspectives on Historical Writing*, edited by Peter Burke, 206–32. Cambridge, UK: Polity Press.

Postrel, Virginia. 1999. "The Pleasures of Persuasion." *Wall Street Journal*, August 2, A18.

Potts, Jason. 2006. "How Creative Are the Super-Rich?" *Agenda* 13 (4): 339–50.

Power, Marcus. 2007. "Digitized Virtuosity: Video War Games and Post-9/11 Cyber-Deterrence." *Security Dialogue* 38 (2): 271–88.

President's Committee on Arts and the Humanities. 2010. "Creative Economy." Available at http://www.pcah.gov/creative-economy.

Project on Student Debt. 2011. "Student Debt and the Class of 2010." Available at http://projectonstudentdebt.org/files/pub/classof2010.pdf.

Pynchon, Thomas. 1984. "Is It O.K. to Be a Luddite?" *New York Times Book Review*, October 28, 1, 40–41.

Rajagopal, Arvind. 2002. "Violence of Commodity Aesthetics: Hawkers, Demolition Raids and a New Regime of Consumption." *Economic and Political Weekly*, January 5–11, 65–67, 69–76.

Ramanathan, Sharada. 2006. "The Creativity Mantra." *The Hindu*, October 29. Available at http://www.hindu.com/mag/2006/10/29/stories/2006102900290700.htm.

Rauch, Alan. 2010. "The Scholarly Journal: Hindsight toward a Digital Future." *Journal of Scholarly Publishing* 42 (1): 56–67.

Reagan, Ronald. 1966. "The Creative Society." Speech at the University of Southern California, April 19. Available at http://www.freerepublic.com/focus/news/742041/posts.

"The Real Housewives of Game Development." 2011. IGN, May 2. Available at http://games.ign.com/articles/116/1165197p1.html.

Rhoades, Gary, and Sheila Slaughter. 1998. "Academic Capitalism, Managed Professionals, and Supply-Side Higher Education." In *Chalk Lines: The Politics of Work in the Managed University*, edited by Randy Martin, 33–68. Durham, NC: Duke University Press.

Ricketts, Glenn, Peter W. Wood, Stephen H. Balch, and Ashley Thorne. 2011. *The Vanishing West 1964–2010: The Disappearance of Western Civilization from the American Undergraduate Curriculum*. Washington, DC: National Association of Scholars.

Ritzer, George, and Nathan Jurgenson. 2010. "Production, Consumption, Prosumption: The Nature of Capitalism in the Age of the Digital 'Prosumer.'" *Journal of Consumer Culture* 10 (1): 13–36.

Roberts, Les, Riyadh Lafta, Richard Garfield, Jamal Khuhairi, and Gilbert Burnham. 2004. "Mortality before and after the 2003 Invasion of Iraq: Cluster Sample Survey." *The Lancet* 364:1857–64.

Rorty, Richard. 1994. "Tales of Two Disciplines." *Callaloo* 17 (2): 575–85.

———. 2006. "The Humanistic Intellectual: Eleven Theses." *Kritikos* 3. Available at http://intertheory.org/rorty.htm.

Ross, Andrew. 2006–2007. "Nice Work If You Can Get It: The Mercurial Career of Creative Industries Policy." *Work Organisation, Labour and Globalisation* 1 (1): 1–19.

———. 2008. "The Offshore Model of Universities." *Liberal Education* 94 (4): 34–39.

———. 2010. "The Corporate Analogy Unravels." *Chronicle of Higher Education*, October 17. Available at http://chronicle.com/article/Farewell-to-the-Corporate/124919.

Rothkopf, David. 1997. "In Praise of Cultural Imperialism." *Foreign Policy* 107:38–53.

"Ruses to Cut Printing Costs." 2010. *The Economist*, September 4, Monitor9.

Said, Edward. 1994. "Identity, Authority, and Freedom: The Potentate and the Traveler." *Boundary 2* 21 (3): 1–18.

Schelling, Felix E. 1914. "New Humanities for Old." *Classical Weekly* 7 (23): 179–84.

Schiller, Dan. 2007. *How to Think about Information*. Urbana: University of Illinois Press.

Schiller, Herbert I. 1976. *Communication and Cultural Domination*. New York: International Arts and Sciences Press.

Schumacher, Leif. 2006–2007. "Immaterial Fordism: The Paradox of Game Industry Labor." *Work Organisation, Labour and Globalisation* 1 (1): 144–55.

Seiter, Ellen. 2005. *The Internet Playground: Children's Access, Entertainment, and Mis-education*. New York: Peter Lang.

"7 Essential Skills You Didn't Learn in College." 2010. *Wired*, October. Available at http://www.wired.com/magazine/2010/09/ff_wiredu.

Shactman, Noah. 2002. "Shoot 'Em Up and Join the Army." *Wired*, July 4. Available at http://www.wired.com/gaming/gamingreviews/news/2002/07/53663.

———. 2010. "Green Monster." *Foreign Policy* (May–June). Available at http://www.foreignpolicy.com/articles/2010/04/26/green_monster?page=full.

Shepherd, Jessica. 2011. "Universities Admit 'Soft' A-Levels Damage Chance of Top Places." *The Guardian*, February 4. Available at http://www.guardian.co.uk/education/2011/feb/04/university-places-traditional-subjects-a-levels.

Silver, David, and Alice Marwick. 2006. "Internet Studies in Times of Terror." In *Critical Cyberculture Studies*, edited by David Silver and Adrienne Massanari, 47–54. New York: New York University Press.

Simpson, Christopher, ed. 1998. *Universities and Empire: Money and Politics in the Social Sciences during the Cold War.* New York: New Press.

Singer, Peter W. 2010. "Meet the Sims . . . and Shoot Them." *Foreign Policy* (March–April). Available at http://www.foreignpolicy.com/articles/2010/02/22/meet_the_sims_and_shoot_them?page=full.

Siva, Nayanah. 2007. "Reed Elsevier to Stop Hosting Exhibitions after Wide Protests." *British Medical Journal* 334 (June): 1182.

Siwek, Stephen E. 2006. *Copyright Industries in the U.S. Economy.* Washington, DC: International Intellectual Property Alliance. Available at http://www.iipa.com/pdf/2006_siwek_full.pdf.

Skerritt, Jane. 2011. "London Metropolitan University: Crimes against Humanities." *openDemocracy*, May 6. Available at http://www.opendemocracy.net/ourkingdom/jane-skerritt/london-metropolitan-university-crimes-against-humanities.

Skorton, David J. 2011. "Don't Cut Humanities." *Washington Post*, February 10. Available at http://voices.washingtonpost.com/college-inc/2011/02/cornells_skorton_dont_cut_huma.html.

Smith, Richard. 2007. "Reed-Elsevier's Hypocrisy in Selling Arms and Health." *Journal of the Royal Society of Medicine* 100:1–2.

Snow, C. P. 1987. *The Two Cultures and a Second Look: An Expanded Version of the Two Cultures and the Scientific Revolution.* Cambridge: Cambridge University Press.

Snowdon, Graham. 2010. "What to Do with a Degree in Media Studies." *The Guardian*, April 24. Available at http://www.guardian.co.uk/money/2010/apr/24/degree-media-studies.

Social Science Research Council. 2007. "SSRC Receives $1.5 Million Ford Grant to Continue Innovative Work on Media Reform." Available at http://www.ssrc.org/press-releases/view/356/.

Solomon, Deborah. 2009. "Questions for Mark Yudof: Big Man on Campus." *New York Times Magazine*, September 24. Available at http://www.nytimes.com/2009/09/27/magazine/27fob-q4-t.html.

Solon. 1994. "I Made the Crooked Straight." In *Citizenship*, edited by Paul Barry Clarke, 38–39. London: Pluto Press.

Sparks, Erin, and Mary Jo Waits. 2011. *Degrees for What Jobs? Raising Expectations for Universities and Colleges in a Global Economy.* Washington, DC: National Governors Association Center for Best Practices.

Standing, Guy. 2011. *The Precariat: The New Dangerous Class.* London: Bloomsbury Academic.

State Public Interest Research Groups. 2005. *Ripoff 101: How the Publishing Industry's Practices Needlessly Drive Up Textbook Costs: A National Survey of Textbook Prices.* 2nd ed. Washington, DC: State Public Interest Research Groups.

Stewart, Debra W., and Kurt M. Landgraf. 2010. "Letter." In *The Path Forward: The Future of Graduate Education in the United States*, by Cathy Wendler, Brent Bridgeman, Fred Cline, Catherine Millett, JoAnn Rock, Nathan Bell, and Patricia McAllister. Princeton, NJ: Educational Testing Service.

Stockwell, Stephen, and Adam Muir. 2003. "The Military-Entertainment Complex: A New Facet of Information Warfare." *Fibreculture* 1. Available at http://one.fibreculturejournal.org/fcj-004-the-military-entertainment-complex-a-new-facet-of-information-warfare.

Striphas, Ted. 2009. *The Late Age of Print: Everyday Book Culture from Consumerism to Control.* New York: Columbia University Press.

Surette, Tim. 2006. "EA Settles OT Dispute, Disgruntled 'Spouse' Outed." *GameSpot*, April 26. Available at http://www.gamespot.com/news/6148369.html.

Sussman, Steve, Mary Ann Pentz, Donna Sprujit-Metz, and Toby Miller. 2006. "Misuse of 'Study Drugs': Prevalence, Consequences, and Implications for Policy." *Substance Abuse Treatment, Prevention, and Policy* 1 (15). Available at http://www.substanceabusepolicy.com/content/1/1/15.

———. 2007a. "Misuse of 'Study Drugs': Prevalence, Consequences, and Implications for Policy." *Journal of Drug Addiction, Education and Eradication* 2 (3–4): 309–27.

———. 2007b. "Misuse of 'Study Drugs': Prevalence, Consequences, and Implications for Policy." In *Trends in Substance Abuse*, edited by Cailin R. McKenna, 133–50. Hauppauge: Nova.

Swain, Harriet. 2011. "London Met VC Explains Why He Is Cutting 400 Courses." *The Guardian*, May 3. Available at http://www.guardian.co.uk/education/2011/may/03/london-metropolitan-gillies-course-cuts.

Szeman, Imre. 2003. "Culture and Globalization, or, the Humanities in Ruins." *CR: The New Centennial Review* 3 (2): 91–115.

Tenner, Edward. 2010. "The Humanities in the Marketplace: Major Misconceptions?" *Atlantic Monthly*, October 13. Available at http://www.theatlantic.com/national/archive/2010/10/the-humanities-in-the-marketplace-major-misconceptions/64458.

Tepper, Steven Jay. 2002. "Creative Assets and the Changing Economy." *Journal of Arts Management, Law and Society* 32 (2): 159–68.

Thompson, Clive. 2004. "The Making of an X Box Warrior." *New York Times Magazine*, August 22. Available at http://query.nytimes.com/gst/fullpage .html?res=9C02EEDD133FF931A1575BC0A9629C8B63&pagewanted=1.

Toffler, Alvin. 1983. *Previews and Premises*. New York: William Morrow.

Tötösy de Zepetnek, Steven. 2010. "The 'Impact Factor' and Selected Issues of Content and Technology in Humanities Scholarship Published Online." *Journal of Scholarly Publishing* 42 (1): 70–78.

Towse, Ruth. 2002. "Review of Richard E. Caves, *Creative Industries: Contracts between Art and Commerce*." *Journal of Political Economy* 110 (1): 234–63.

Tuchman, Gaye. 2009. *Wannabe U: Inside the Corporate University*. Chicago: University of Chicago Press.

Turner, Graeme. 2007. "Another Way of Looking at It." *The Australian*, May 30. Available at http://www.theaustralian.com.au/higher-education/another- way-of-looking-at-it/story-e6frgcjx-1111113636658.

———. 2012. *What's Become of Cultural Studies?* London: Sage.

Turse, Nick. 2008. *The Complex: How the Military Invades Our Everyday Lives*. New York: Metropolitan Books.

"Undercover Boss: Awards and Nominations." 2012. Emmys. Available at http://www.emmys.com/shows/undercover-boss.

Ungar, Sanford J. 2010. "7 Major Misperceptions about the Liberal Arts." *Chronicle of Higher Education*, February 28. Available at http://chronicle .com/article/7-Major-Misperceptions-About/64363.

United Nations. 2004. "Creative Industries and Development." United Nations Conference on Trade and Development, eleventh session, São Paolo, Brazil, June 13–18. Available at http://www.unctad.org/en/docs/tdxibpd13 _en.pdf.

United Nations Educational, Scientific and Cultural Organization. 1955. "The Role of the Humanities in Contemporary Culture: Basic Paper." Available at http://unesdoc.unesco.org/images/0017/001797/179701eb.pdf.

———. 2002. *Culture and UNESCO*. Paris: UNESCO.

United States Atomic Energy Commission. 1954. "In the Matter of J. Robert Oppenheimer." Transcript of hearing before Personnel Security Board. Available at http://universityhonors.umd.edu/HONR269J/archive/AEC54 0612.htm.

United States Census Bureau. 2011. "Overview of Race and Hispanic Origin: 2010." Available at http://www.census.gov/prod/cen2010/briefs/ c2010br-02.pdf.

University of New South Wales. 2012. "School of Humanities and Social Sciences (HASS): Disciplines." Available at http://hass.unsw.adfa.edu.au/ disciplines.html.

Valdivia, Angharad. 2001. "Rhythm Is Gonna Get You! Teaching Evaluations and the Feminist Multicultural Classroom." *Feminist Media Studies* 1 (3): 387–89.

Vincent, Norah. 2000. "Hop on Pop: Lear, Seinfeld, and the Dumbing Down of the Academy." *Village Voice*, February 1. Available at http://www.village voice.com/2000-02-01/nyc-life/hop-on-pop.

Waltham, Mary. 2010. "The Future of Scholarly Journal Publishing among Social Science and Humanities Associations." *Journal of Scholarly Publishing* 41 (3): 257–324.

Wang, Yanlai. 2003. *China's Economic Development and Democratization.* Farnham, UK: Ashgate.

Ware, Mark, and Michael Mabe. 2009. *The STM Report: An Overview of Scientific and Scholarly Publishing.* Oxford, UK: International Association of Scientific, Technical and Medical Publishers.

Waters, Darren. 2007. "Videogames Industry 'Is Maturing.'" *BBC News*, March 5. Available at http://news.bbc.co.uk/2/hi/technology/6412929.stm.

Weaver, Warren, and Claude Elwood Shannon. 1963. *The Mathematical Theory of Communication.* Urbana: University of Illinois Press.

Weber, Samuel. 2000. "The Future of the Humanities: Experimenting." *Culture Machine* 2. Available at http://www.culturemachine.net/index.php/cm/article/view/311/296.

"What Good Are Economics Journals?" 2011. *The Economist*, March 23. Available at http://www.economist.com/blogs/freeexchange/2011/03/econom ics_3.

Whittam Smith, Andreas. 2008. "Media Studies Is No Preparation for Journalism." *The Independent*, February 25.

Wilby, Peter. 2009. "I Sued and Won." *New Statesman*, August 20. Available at http://www.newstatesman.com/uk-politics/2009/08/soft-media-services-britain.

Windschuttle, Keith. 2006. "Communication Breakdown." *The Australian*, June 17.

Winocur, Rosalía. 2002. *Ciudadanos mediáticos: La construcción de lo publico en la radio.* Barcelona: Editorial Gedisa.

Woodhead, Chris. 2009. "Dive for Cover If You See 'Studies': It Means Bogus." *The Times*, March 8, 9.

Woodrow Wilson National Fellowship Foundation. 2004. *Responsive Ph.D.* Princeton, NJ: Woodrow Wilson National Fellowship Foundation. Available at http://www.woodrow.org/images/pdf/resphd/ResponsivePhD_overview .pdf.

Woodward, Kathleen. 2009. "The Future of the Humanities—in the Present and in Public." *Daedalus* 138 (1): 110–23.

Wooster, Harvey A. 1932. "To Unify the Liberal-Arts Curriculum: The Principle of Evolution as a Unifying Concept for the College Curriculum." *Journal of Higher Education* 3 (7): 373–80.

Wright, Matthew. 2010. "Could University Cutbacks Be the Saviour of English?" *The Guardian*, December 16. Available at http://www.guardian.co.uk/commentisfree/2010/dec/29/cutbacks-leavis-english-impact-literary-criticism.

Young, Charles, and Fiona Godlee. 2007. "Reed Elsevier's Arms Trade." *British Medical Journal* 334 (March): 547.

Young, Damon. 2010. "Philosophy as a Contact Sport." *The Australian*, December 8. Available at http://www.theaustralian.com.au/higher-education/opinion-analysis/philosophy-as-a-contact-sport/story-e6frgcko-1225967182548.

Yu, Maochun Miles, Timothy Disher, and Andrew T. Phillips. 2010. "Educating Warriors: Globally Engaged and Culturally Aware." *Liberal Education* 96 (2). Available at http://www.aacu.org/liberaleducation/le-sp10/LESP10_Educating.cfm.

Yu, Pauline. 2006. "Foreword." In *Our Cultural Commonwealth*, by American Council of Learned Societies Commission on Cyberinfrastructure for the Humanities and Social Sciences, i–ii. New York: American Council of Learned Societies.

———. 2008. "An Investment in Value: Support for Research in the Humanities." Lecture given at Academia Sinica, Taipei, Taiwan, March 24. Available at http://www.acls.org/uploadedFiles/Publications/PresTalks/08_Investment_in_Value.pdf.

Yúdice, George. 1990. "For a Practical Aesthetics." *Social Text* 25–26:129–45.

———. 2002. *El recurso de la cultura: Usos de la cultura en la era global.* Barcelona: Editorial Gedisa.

———. 2003. *The Expediency of Culture: Culture as Resource in an Era of Globalization.* Durham, NC: Duke University Press.

Zuckerman, Harriet, and Ronald G. Ehrenberg. 2009. "Recent Trends in Funding for the Academic Humanities and Their Implications." *Daedalus* 138 (1): 124–46.

Index

Brunsdon, Charlotte, 103
Brzezinski, Zbigniew, 68
Burnett, Ron, 71
Bush, George H. W., 6
Bush, George W., 6
Butler, Judith, 103
Byatt, A. S., 49
Byron, Lord, 4

Cabral, Amilcar, 102–103
Campaign against Arms Trade, 49
Campbell, Marion, 122n
Canclini, Néstor García, 71, 103–104, 106
Carey, James, 71
Césaire, Aimé, 102
Chakravartty, Paula, 71
Chartier, Roger, 105
Chomsky, Noam, 21
Christian Science Monitor, 118
Cicero, 65
Citizenship, 3, 42–44, 114
Classics, 33–37
Close, Chuck, 6
Coetzee, J. M., 49
Cognitariat, 79, 82, 88–92
Cohen, Nick, 46
Coleridge, Samuel Taylor, 32–33
Commission on the Humanities and Social
    Sciences, 6
Council for the Humanities, Arts and
    Social Sciences (Australia), 29, 79
Creative industries, 63–92
Cultural policy studies, 70–72, 104
Cultural studies, 93–116
Culture, 31–34
Cunningham, Stuart, 70–71, 73–74, 95,
    103, 122n
Curtin, Mike, 72

Dames, Nicholas, 11
Darling, John, 122n
Davidson, Cathy N., 67
DeLillo, Don, 93
Digital Millennium Copyright Act, 57–58
Diogenes, 30
Dissent, 110–111
Donoghue, Frank, 45
Dorfman, Ariel, 102

Dorland, Michael, 71
Durkheim, Émile, 10
Dutton, Michael, 122n
Dyson, Esther, 77

ea_spouse, 90–91
EastEnders, 4, 112
Eco, Umberto, 21, 57–58
Edgar, David, 63
Eisenhower, Dwight D., 4–5, 83
Electronic Arts (EA), 89–92
Else, Gerald F., 35–36
Elsevier, 48–49
Emerson, Ralph Waldo, 66n
Engels, Frederick, 10, 38
Erving, Julius, 90
European Commission, 29
European Science Foundation, 10
Europeans for Medical Progress, 49
European Union, 115

Facebook, 9, 81
Fanon, Frantz, 102–103
Felski, Rita, 122n
Ferguson, Charles, 50
Ferris Bueller's Day Off, 42
FIFA World Cup, 89
Fiske, John, 103, 122n
Fitzgerald, F. Scott, 58
Florida, Richard, 77–78, 81, 91
Fortune, 91
Foucault, Michel, 10, 31, 103, 118
Freire, Bianca, 71
Freire, Paolo, 103
Freire Filho, João, 71
Freud, Sigmund, 10
Frow, John, 122n
Fulbright, J. William, 83
Full Metal Jacket, 37
Full Spectrum Warrior, 84

Games, 82–92
Gamespot PC Reviews, 85
Garfinkel, Harold, 21
Gates, Kelly, 72
Gates, Robert, 38–39
Geiger, Roger, 1, 6
Gellner, Ernest, 65

Toby Miller is Distinguished Professor of Media and Cultural Studies at the University of California, Riverside. He is author of *Sportsex* and *Cultural Citizenship: Cosmopolitanism, Consumerism, and Television in a Neoliberal Age* (both Temple) and runs the *culturalstudies* podcast.